A Rainbow
of Saris

*Four true stories
of missionary women in India*

Edited by Janice Kerper Brauer

International Lutheran Women's Missionary League
St. Louis, Missouri

Contents

Acknowledgements

The story of "Hanna's Children" is taken from the family history collected by Mathilda Lutz Weber; correspondence files of The Lutheran Church—Missouri Synod Mission Board in the Concordia Historical Institute, St. Louis, Missouri; memories of Juanita Lutz and Alice and Elizabeth Paul; and interviews with various former India missionaries.

Most of Angela Rehwinkel's story comes from correspondence in the Mission Board files at the Concordia Historical Institute. Former missionaries who knew her and members of her family have also supplied anecdotes and pictures.

Mary Esther Otten's story is based on letters and photographs provided by her sons David and Joel.

In addition, author Louise Mueller has drawn information from the following books:

Among the Palms in India, Louise C. Rathke, Mennonite Press, Newton, Kansas, 1977

A Century in the Madura Mission, Harriet Wilder, Vantage Press, New York, 1967

A Chance to Die, The Life and Legacy of Amy Carmichael, Elisabeth Elliot, Fleming H. Revell Co., Old Tappan, New Jersey, 1987

A Church in Mission, Identity and Purpose in India, Luther H. Meinzen, Printed in India at the Concordia Press and Training Institute, Vaniyambadi, 1981

Dr. Ida, The Story of Ida Scudder of Vellore, Dorothy Clarke Wilson, McGraw Hill, New York, 1959

The Gold Cord, Amy Carmichael, SPCK, London, MacMillan Co., Printed in Great Britain, 1934, 1937, 1943, 1947, 1957

Much Cause for Joy, Herbert M. Zorn, Missouri Evangelical India Mission, Malappuram, Kerala, 1970

Snake Temple, An Indian Diary, H. Earl Miller, Carlton Press, Inc., New York, 1977

Foreword

When a female missionary from India shares her experiences with American audiences, she often wears a sari, the traditional dress of Indian women. Sometimes she calls for a volunteer and demonstrates how the yards of beautiful cloth are draped to create this graceful garment.

Like the saris they wore — some colorful and bright, some plain and drab, some of finest silk, others of coarsely woven cotton — missionary women in India made up a rainbow of personalities, lifestyles and ministries.

This book began from an idea to honor Rose Ziemke, who served in India for some 30 years, on her 50th anniversary as a deaconess in The Lutheran Church–Missouri Synod (LCMS). Rose was presented with a partially funded "homecoming" trip back to India, on which I was privileged to accompany her. Everywhere we went — worship services at various congregations, familiar shops where she used to buy merchandise, various towns where she worked — people remembered her, were glad to see her and praised her. Rose took all this attention graciously and directed the glory to Jesus Christ. Rose tells her own story in "In India Where Roses Bloom."

Like Rose, the other women whose stories are told here touched many lives through their work in India. "Hanna's Children," by Louise Mueller, traces women from four generations of the Lutz family. "Angela of Mercy," also by Louise, tells the story of Nurse Angela Rehwinkel, who faithfully served in medical missions in India for nearly 40 years. Author Ruby Young pored over letters written from Hank and Mary Esther Otten to friends in the United States and recaptures that story in "Mary Esther's Mission."

The Lutheran Women's Missionary League joyfully presents this book to The Lutheran Church–Missouri Synod in celebration of 150 years since the denomination's founding and with thankfulness to the Lord for 100 years of LCMS foreign mission work, which began in India.

Suzanne Sears
November 1995

6

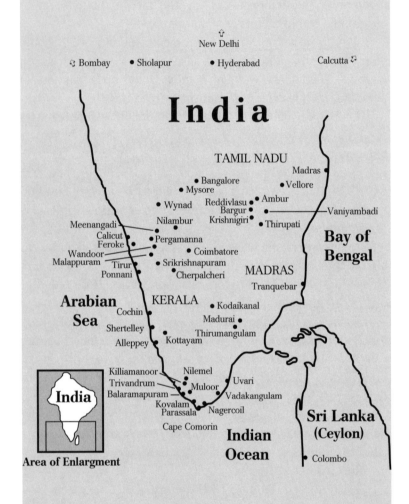

New Delhi

꒯ Bombay   ● Sholapur   ● Hyderabad   Calcutta ꒯

India

TAMIL NADU
                                    Madras ●
                ● Bangalore   ● Vellore
              ● Mysore
         ● Wynad   Reddivlasu ● ● Ambur
              Nilambur   Bargur ●   ●——— Vaniyambadi
Meenangadi   Krishnigiri ● Thirupati
  Calicut
  Feroke   ● Pergamanna   **Bay of**
Wandoor   ● Coimbatore   **Bengal**
Malappuram Tirur ● Srikrishnapuram
  Ponnani   ˙Cherpalcheri   MADRAS

Arabian   KERALA   ● Kodaikanal   Tranquebar ●
Sea   Cochin   Madurai ●
   Shertelley   Thirumangulam
   Alleppey   ● Kottayam

      Killiamanoor   Nilemel
      Trivandrum——   ● Muloor   Uvari
      Balaramapuram—— ● ●Vadakangulam
        Kovalam Nagercoil   **Sri Lanka**
        Parassala   **(Ceylon)**
        Cape Comorin   **Indian**
                        Ocean   ● Colombo

Area of Enlargment

Hanna's Children

by Louise Mueller

Elizabeth — 1995

"India was great!" Elizabeth tosses her red hair; her large brown eyes sparkle.

"What was special about living there?" I ask this petite high school senior.

"I loved it! I loved the Indian people and their traditions and the country — and everything," she replies. "We lived at Kodaikanal, up in the hills where it never got really hot or really cold, and it was so beautiful! The people are so neat, and their customs and festivals are so colorful.

"There were big parades. We'd heard wild stories about kids being kidnapped during such events, and we were scared but fascinated as we peeked through the bushes to watch. I remember a festival where the men would take a big fishhook and put it through their skins and hang themselves from poles to be carried around. That was the weirdest! And they always had fireworks — fireworks for Christmas, fireworks for New Years, fireworks for religious festivals.

"At the festival where I met my best friend, they give presents to everybody; it's sort of like Christmas, but it's a Hindu festival. We were down on the plains visiting a maharajah, kind of a king. My dad was friends with his brother, so they invited us for one of the celebrations. Rama and her family were there at the same time, so we met and just started talking and playing. Later her mother rented one of the houses on our property, and she went to school at Kodaikanal International School. Her dad was a sea captain, so he was hardly ever home. We always had fun and became best friends. I haven't seen her for seven years, but I still write to her.

"Then there was a girl from Australia — her parents were volunteer teachers at the Kodaikanal school where my mom and dad were houseparents. I still write to her too. Last summer her family was making a tour of the United States and came to visit us. It was neat!

"I was five years old when we moved to India. We lived in the Loch End Lutheran boarding school, which really was a huge sort of mansion. The first few years I stayed with my parents. They had an apartment on the first floor. When I was seven or eight, I moved upstairs and roomed with other girls. First grade was in the school building on Loch End property; for second and third grade I took a bus to a place called Swedish House, about five miles away. And fourth grade was across the street on the Kodaikanal International School property. They were all connected to the one school.

"My Grandma and Grandpa Lutz were living in India then too. I knew that my grandfather and great-grandfather were missionaries to India, that my mom had been born there, and that my sister was born there. But it really hadn't occurred to me that we're the fourth generation of Lutz women to live in India. I wasn't conscious of being part of the history of The Lutheran Church—Missouri Synod overseas missions, but I'm proud that we've been a part of bringing Christianity to India.

"I never knew my great-grandmother, Hanna Lutz. She died before my mother was born. It would be fun to know what kind of a person she really was!"

I. Hanna

Hanna could not remember the first time she crossed the ocean by boat. She was only one month old when her immigrant parents left Waldeck, Germany, to come to the United States. Twenty years later she set out across the same ocean on another ship. It was 1913. Johanna Christina Scherer was en route to join her missionary fiancé, Anton Lutz, who had preceded her to India one year earlier. At that

Johanna (Hanna) Scherer Lutz

time single men were required to work overseas one year, to see if they could tolerate the climate and culture, before their sweethearts were allowed to join them. Nurse Lula Ellermann, the first medical missionary of The Lutheran Church—Missouri Synod (LCMS) was her cabin-mate. Four new bachelor missionaries were their escorts. Carefully folded in Hanna's baggage were the traditional white wedding dress and veil.

During those long days on the rolling ship, surrounded by the waves of the great Atlantic Ocean, Hanna could identify with the loneliness and heartache her mother must have felt as she traveled farther and farther away from the home and family she would never see again. Hanna consoled herself that she was not leaving forever; Anton's tour of duty would end, and they would return to the United States and her home in St. Louis, Missouri.

Christianity in India

Legend claims the Apostle Thomas brought Christianity to India. Christians greeted Vasco da Gama in 1498 when he had successfully sailed around Africa and found a sea route to India for the Portuguese king. In the 16th century, the Jesuit priest Francis Xavier established a strong Catholic community among the fisher folk on the southern coast of India. German Lutheran missionary Bartholomew Ziegenbalg, who arrived in India in 1706 sponsored by the Danish king Frederick IV, translated the New Testament and part of the Old Testament into the Tamil language.

In 1846 Eduard Baierlein, originally slated for the Leipzig Mission field in India but prevented from going by ill health, came to the United States to work among the Chippewa Indians in Michigan. In 1851 he accepted a renewed appointment to India and served there for 33 years. He took with him the interest and support of his friends and colleagues in the United States. In 1883 when India missionaries Karl Naether and Franz Mohn were expelled from the Leipzig Mission because of their protests against German liberalism, the

American Lutherans were ready to act. Both men were invited to the United States where they were examined, accepted into membership, and in 1894 commissioned to go to India as the first foreign missionaries of The Lutheran Church—Missouri Synod (LCMS).

Anton Lutz, one of the synod's first American-born missionaries, was sent to Nagercoil, on the southern tip of India, to work among the Tamil-speaking people.

The End of the Journey

Hanna was overwhelmed by the sights, sounds and smells of India. The shrill cries of the hawkers and street urchins, the trumpeting of elephants, the constant rumbling of oxcarts and the shuffling of feet on the streets caused an incessant humming in her ears (she was partially deaf as a result of scarlet fever). The smells of unwashed perspiring bodies, of animal and human feces carelessly dropped on the thoroughfares, and the odors of pungent spices and incense assaulted her nostrils. She recoiled at the ragged beggars huddled in the sparse shade near the mud huts, the emaciated dogs and cows that wandered at will, the dust raised by the constant milling of people. But Hanna reveled in the profusion of lush tropical foliage and flowers and her first sight of palm trees.

How shocked she was to see Anton looking so pale and thin! He had been ill for much of his first year in India. But as he greeted his fiancee he exclaimed joyfully, "The sight of you makes me better already!"

The last 50 miles of Hanna's journey were on a straw-filled oxcart, a bumpy overnight trip with frequent delays while the caravan waited for fresh bullocks. Once during the night Anton, riding behind Hanna on the baggage cart, woke just in time to see one of the bullocks, chewing the straw on which Hanna was sleeping, about to take a bite of his sleeping fiancee's black hair.

Housekeeping in India

Hanna married and began housekeeping in a typical South India bungalow made of sun-dried bricks with a tile roof and cement floor. The mat-roofed veranda along the front of the house provided shade for the rooms and a place for children to play. The kitchen was a separate hut, 30 feet from the main house; the heat of the wood-burning stove would have been intolerable had it been closer. But in a driving rain the meal might arrive sodden and inedible. A covered walkway was added to the bungalows later built especially for the missionaries.

Windows were barred but had no screens; they did not keep out scampering lizards, bugs, insects — or snakes! One night Hanna latched the front door in the dark, having forgotten to do so before retiring. Next morning she found a cobra caught in the doorway, its head inside. That was a close call — she had been barefoot and the latch pushed down at floor level.

In establishing mission work in India, the American Lutheran missionaries learned from the experiences of earlier missions. They realized that if their workers were to be effective and remain for any length of time, their health needed to be safeguarded. Two of Karl Naether's children had died of dysentery within a few days of each other; Naether himself had succumbed to plague. In the early 1900s there were no antibiotics. Mosquitoes carried malaria, wounds quickly became infected and produced blood poisoning. Europeans had not built up generations of immunity to virulent tropical diseases.

Hanna knew of these past tragedies, and guarding her family's health was a great priority. She had learned "scrubby-Dutch" cleanliness in German South St. Louis, and she was a well-organized manager. She was also adaptable and could make adjustments to the primitive tropical environment. The number of people she was responsible for steadily increased — eight children were born in the span of 14 years. A tribute to her efforts is that they remained healthy with no serious illnesses or life-threatening accidents.

Cholera immunizations were an annual occurrence; the older children took worm medicine every year before going off to boarding school. Fresh fruit and produce were washed in a solution of potassium permanganate. Drinking water was boiled and stored in *goosas*, clay jugs that kept the water cool. The children were warned against playing with children who might have lice and "itch." When they left the shade of the veranda they were required to wear *topees* (pith helmets) and were not allowed out of the house during the heat of the day. Hanna donned a *topee* when she went to the kitchen to supervise the cooking and baking. There was a superstition that if white people went out in the sun with their heads uncovered their brains would liquify!

One day a woman with elephantiasis, an enlargement of the lower extremities, came to beg. She had a child along, and Hanna's second daughter went out to play with her. Hanna called Mathilda inside and sharply chided her about exposing herself to disease. This frightened the child into believing she would get elephantiasis. Assuming that the germs would enter through her feet, she thought, "My feet can't swell if I wear my shoes to bed." And for some weeks she did just that.

Servants in India took the place of conveniences and appliances available in the United States. Even though the missionaries had to budget carefully and sometimes depend on financial help from relatives, they were wealthy by Indian standards. Amid abject poverty and starvation, it was considered selfish not to employ those less fortunate. The Lutzes kept three full-time servants: a cook, a gardener/errand boy and an *ayah* (baby sitter).

Joseph, the cook, was responsible for boiling and cooling sufficient water for drinking. He came every morning to consult with "Madam" about the day's menu. There was no running water, no electricity, no refrigeration. Everything was cooked from scratch. Meat, fruit and produce had to be purchased daily at the market. Most European women did not go to the marketplace; besides Hanna would have had difficulty bargaining with the merchants. So Joseph made the journey, walking the mile or more. Sometimes he paid a coolie to carry the loaded basket, deftly balanced on his head, back to the house. Hanna baked all the family's bread after the cook had cleaned the wheat and taken it to the mill for grinding. Some adjustments had to be made in cooking. Rice was substituted for potatoes; mutton, chicken and fish replaced beef. Mangos, guavas, papayas, plantain, coconuts and other tropical fruits were plentiful.

Samidos, the gardener, had the primary task of carrying water from the well in two large containers attached to a pole carried on his shoulders. He had to satisfy all the needs of the home: water for bathing, for washing clothes, for kitchen needs, and for the garden and potted plants. He was also often called on to run errands, and he helped Joseph in the kitchen.

Annamal, the *ayah*, helped with the house cleaning and watched the children. One never knew when little feet would wander beyond the veranda or out into the busy street. Curious little fingers would not know that a hole in the ground might house a snake.

There was also a *dhoby* who came weekly to do laundry, pounding the clothes on rocks along the stream, and a sweeper who came daily to clean the commodes. Such work was below the caste of the *ayahs*; they would rinse out the babies' wet diapers, but some of them refused to touch the soiled ones.

Hanna sewed all the children's clothes except for those sent from ladies' societies in the United States and those often needed re-sizing. When the work piled up she would hire a tailor.

Servants were a necessary burden to Hanna. Her deafness made it difficult for her to learn the Tamil language; she never mastered more than was necessary for basic communication. Since she could not hear all that was said, she was often frustrated and suspicious. She always checked the cook's purchases carefully and put everything not used immediately into a locked storeroom. The keys were on a ring fastened to her belt with a large safety pin. Hanna's children, on the other hand, considered all the servants members of the family. Although bland American food was served at the family table, the children loved to sample the spicy dishes Joseph prepared for the servants. They followed Samidos around as he did his errands; they chattered with Annamal in Tamil.

German Lutherans

Every evening Hanna gathered the children around her chair and listened to their prayers. One of the first prayers she taught the little ones was (translated from German): "I am little; my heart make clean. Allow no one to live within save Jesus alone." German was the language of the LCMS at that time; the missionaries wrote reports and papers in German, conversed with one another in German and spoke German in their homes.

When World War I broke out in 1914, the English government rounded up the Germans in India and sent them back to their homeland in exchange for British prisoners of war. Sometimes mission property was confiscated. The ranks of Lutheran missionaries were sadly depleted. Hanna received a letter ordering her to leave in 14 days. Anton appealed to the American Consul in Madras with proof that his wife was an American citizen, and she received a letter of apology from the British Resident.

Missionary Wife

To establish the Christian church in India, missionaries travelled to villages in their areas. Often they arrived early in the day, before the men went to work, and gathered an audience at a road intersection. If there was already a Christian presence, they arranged for regular visits and helped organize small congregations. The villages were usually fairly close together, but for the early missionaries the only mode of transportation was walking or riding in a cart drawn by bullocks.

Even a few miles meant jolting on primitive roads or walking dusty paths in tropical heat; both were painfully slow.

After a few years Anton was provided with a "Red Indian" motorcycle. The side car was a large wicker basket. Anton would occasionally take his family for a ride, Hanna in the side basket with one child at her feet and another in her arms, another seated on the luggage carrier and a fourth on the handle bars. Anton used the motorcycle to reach the preaching stations he served and the Lutheran mission's boarding school for boys in Nagercoil, where he was a teacher.

In Vadakangulam, 12 miles from Nagercoil, there was a large and thriving Catholic church composed of two Indian castes, the Vellalas and the Nadars. A wall down the center of the church separated them until a zealous Belgian priest, sent to be their new pastor, decreed the dividing wall be removed. The Vellalas walked out in protest and formed an independent congregation. Endeavoring to find another Christian denomination that taught in accord with their Tamil Bible, they sent emissaries to the Lutheran mission in Nagercoil, and Anton Lutz was asked to be their pastor. But he must promise not to force them to admit lower caste members into the congregation or even allow them to attend services. "I'll promise not to force you to do anything," Anton replied, "but in turn you must promise you will listen to what I have to say about caste distinction."

Mission bungalow at Vadakangulam

Since the congregation at Vadakangulam was already established and was nearer Anton's preaching stations, the Mission Board built a bungalow/compound there and the Lutzes moved. Anton had been raised on a farm and had an analytical mind. He designed and supervised building the new home. Instead of being built in a square, five spacious rooms were strung out in a row, giving cross ventilation, with verandas along the front and back. His house plan also included kiln-dried bricks at the bottom and top of the walls to keep out white ants. This became the pattern for future missionary homes.

Around the property — always called a compound, even if there was only one house on it — was a low wall of sun-dried bricks. On rural compounds it was sometimes a cactus hedge. The walls were not intended to keep out people, just animals. The Indian people are innately courteous but also curious, and once in a while a missionary would awaken to see a pair of dark eyes staring though the window bars. Beggars came to the bungalow, and Anton never turned one away. Hanna too was sympathetic, and her veranda was often the dispensary for food and simple medicines.

At Uvari, a coastal fishing village some 42 miles from Vadakangulam, the Christians were descendants of Saint Francis Xavier's converts of the 1500s. An ambitious Catholic priest demanded one day's catch of fish every week for the church. Some of the members protested and broke away, forming an Anglican congregation. The priest did not give up his parishioners easily; fighting and litigation followed. The Anglican Church decided to withdraw, and the breakaway group began looking elsewhere for a pastor. In 1919 a Lutheran congregation was established and Anton served there also, making the trip about once a month. The bad feelings continued, and members of the congregation would meet Anton where he left his motorcycle, walking with him the last two miles across the sand to ensure his safety.

One Sunday Hanna was ill, and Anton had to cancel the trip to Uvari. The next day he went there and found the village in great disorder. Houses were wrecked and police were standing around. There had been a riot the day before, and several villagers had been killed. The riot had been timed to coincide with Anton's arrival; he was the intended victim. Hanna had felt distressed that Anton had neglected his work for her, but her illness had actually saved his life. Knowing her husband would continue to visit Uvari, she was not completely comforted.

Hanna felt lonely and isolated living on the Vadakangulam compound, away from other missionary wives with only small children to keep her company. Anton was dedicated to his ministry and was away from home serving his far-flung parishes at least 60 percent of the time. One of his letters to the Mission Board defined his many tasks as "lawyer, contractor, carpenter, mason, architect, motor mechanic, treasurer, cashier, accountant, supervisor of schools, preacher, teacher, *seelsorger* [soul saver] and ...." His intensity and complete commitment often pushed him beyond his physical strength; with exhaustion came discouragement and depression. Hanna's quiet orderliness and gracious serenity were the balance he needed.

The birth of Hanna's fifth child, Mildred, was followed by severe hemorrhaging. Dr. Noble at the Salvation Army Hospital in Nagercoil did not think Hanna would live until morning. All through the night Anton sat at her bedside, whispering prayers into her good ear. Next morning the doctor exclaimed with much emotion, "Your prayers have saved her!" She was still weak, and Anton cared for her tenderly during her slow recovery. He also fed and changed the baby and supervised the other children.

First Furlough

Almost nine years passed from when Hanna first arrived in India to her first return to St. Louis. Anton had booked passage on a ship and then received a telegram saying the ship would leave early. He and Hanna packed hurriedly through the night and boarded a train early the next morning to reach the ship. No sooner had they gotten settled than another telegram arrived saying the ship had already sailed. Their baggage was loaded and could not be retrieved, so they went on to the port city of Colombo where Anton managed to find a freighter leaving that evening for Boston. Only one stateroom was available, so the big family was crowded during the long sea journey. A severe storm struck as they crossed the Atlantic; waves washed over the decks, the ship lurched and rolled, furniture had to be bolted down, and the passengers were given life jackets. Baby Mildred took a bad tumble, landing on her head, and later had a mastoid infection. After so many years in the tropics, the family was ill prepared for colder weather and shivered in their "India" clothes; some of the women aboard sewed simple coats from blankets for the children.

When the family finally stumbled off the ship in Boston harbor, exhausted and bedraggled, the pastor who had been assigned to help them through customs was so ashamed of their shabbiness he would not stand in the inspection line with them. To add insult to injury, Anton discovered the currency value had suddenly dropped, and he had to borrow $10 from his grudging host for train fare to St. Louis.

As Anton, Hanna and the five small children boarded the train, they heard their fellow passengers exclaim, "Look at that family! No sleep for us tonight!" Since the Lutzes were speaking German, they were assumed to be immigrants. But the children were so well trained they did not cry out once, not even Mathilda, one of the older daughters, who fell from an upper berth. Next morning when the pullman had been converted back to seats, the other passengers could not contain their curiosity, walking down the aisle to have a look. Finally one man was bold enough to ask, "Who are you anyway?" Anton explained he was a missionary returning from India. Soon most of the passengers in the car came to talk with Hanna and Anton; cookies and candy were shared with the children.

Finally Hanna was home! Of course it was not as large or as grand as memory had painted it, and after so many years her family and friends were older; their lives had gone on without her. But she was able to renew many friendships and enjoyed meeting the next generation of relatives. She had forgotten how hot St. Louis was in summertime. Anton said they might as well be back in India!

Anton lectured at Concordia Seminary about his mission work. The family went to Idaho to visit Anton's family, and Hanna gave birth to her sixth child, Walter. Lydia, the oldest, enrolled in first grade. So imperceptibly they scarcely noticed, the children began speaking English instead of German.

All too soon the year passed, and it was time to return to India. Anton was anxious to resume his work. When the return ship came to shore in Bombay harbor, he took a deep breath and exclaimed, "Ah, the smells of India!" Hanna did not share his enthusiasm. She was facing a far more wrenching parting than when she first left America; it was time for the three older children to go to boarding school. The pattern of separate education for Europeans had long been set by the ruling British. But that did not change the sorrow and loss Hanna felt sending the children away at the tender ages of six, seven and eight.

The School at Kodaikanal

Two hundred miles north of Nagercoil lay the beautiful resort of Kodaikanal, a paradise of green forests, waterfalls, a mountain lake, delightful hiking trails, orchid and rose gardens. In 1913 the Lutheran mission purchased property there, and with funds from women's societies in the United States a third vacation cottage was added to the two existing ones. For six weeks each year, during the worst of the heat, missionary families had a respite in the cooler temperatures 7,000 feet above sea level.

Part of the annual journey was by train. But in earlier years the final climb up the mountain was on foot. Coolies would carry the smaller children and pregnant women in *doolie* chairs (canvas stretchers) as they chanted "O-a-hung-o" at intervals. Later a mountain road was constructed and a bus would negotiate the 30 miles of hairpin curves.

In 1922 a school for missionary children was begun on the Kodaikanal compound. Paul Bachmann and his wife came from the United States to be teacher and houseparents. The three older Lutz children were among the ten original pupils. To make the transition a little easier, Anton scheduled his Kodaikanal vacation to coincide with the beginning of the school year. After a week in the bungalow with the family, Lydia, Mathilda and Arnold moved to the boarding school. The very first evening Lydia spilled her milk. After being made to clean up the mess, she was sent to her room without finishing supper. Not at all used to such stern discipline, she promptly ran down the hill to her mother. It took a lot of gentle urging on Hanna's part to persuade Lydia to return to school.

School was in session nine months of the year. "Summer" vacation was from October to January, so the children were always home for Christmas. A family vacation was arranged in May or June, about midway through the term, and during those weeks the children were permitted to stay with their parents. Each year or so another Lutz child joined his siblings at the Kodaikanal boarding school. The separations did not get easier for Hanna. Every time another child left the nest there was a new hole in her heart.

A Seminary in India

From the beginning the Lutheran mission intended that the Indian churches would eventually be served by Indian pastors and teachers. In Nagercoil there were both a boys' and a girls' boarding school, and laymen were trained as pastoral assistants. Many of the Hindu and Muslim landlords would not rent to Christian missionaries. The Mission Board was able to purchase a lot on which to build the schools cheaply because it was near the hanging place for public executions. The India Evangelical Lutheran Church's Concordia Seminary was later built on adjacent property.

In 1922 a conference of missionaries and lay delegates voted to start a seminary at Nagercoil. Anton was asked to be one of three professors. He hesitated to give up his work in the congregations, which was his first love, but bowed to the wishes and confidence of his associates. With typical concentration he began an in-depth study of theology, spending a vacation in Kodaikanal with a *munshi* (language teacher) so he could better translate references and textbooks for his pupils. The seminary opened in 1924, and four years later the first class of seven Indian pastors graduated.

Caste

The change in responsibilities meant a move back to Nagercoil for the Lutz family. A newly arrived missionary, Erwin Meinzen, took over most of Anton's congregational work. At Vadakangulam a young man of the Panchama caste walked into the church and the entire Vallala congregation walked out. After several weeks of facing empty pews, the novice missionary came to his peers for advice. Most of the men advised him to stand fast — caste was wrong and should not be allowed among Christians. Anton well knew the evils of caste in India. Nonetheless he advocated a more cautious approach, suggesting that Pastor Meinzen talk to the young man and offer to minister to him privately until the other church members, under continued influence of the Gospel, decided to include him. There was a good deal of disagreement and controversy. Some of the missionaries even refused to attend Holy Communion with Anton, but his advice was finally followed. Fifteen years later the Vadakangulam congregation, of its own accord, opened its doors to all castes. In time the bad feelings healed, but the animosity was another heartache for Hanna. Caste remained a difficult challenge for the Indian church.

Family Partings

Hanna's greatest heartache came when Lydia and Mathilda had completed their studies at Kodaikanal and were ready for high school. Now what? Relatives in St. Louis and Idaho had large families and small houses. Should they keep the girls in India for another year? Along with most of his compatriots, Anton believed that European children (especially girls) remaining in India during puberty could not develop properly. Finally there came an offer from Pastor Frederick Schumann and his wife in Salt Lake City, friends of Erwin Meinzen, and in desperation the Lutzes accepted. So in 1928 the two girls set out, escorted as far as New York City by missionary Paul Heckel and his wife. In boarding school the girls had learned to lean on each other, to keep problems and hurts to themselves, and to be self-sufficient. But they looked so small and alone as they said their farewells, Hanna thought her heart would break. She began to count the days until the next furlough; at the same time she dreaded it, knowing the two older boys would remain with their sisters.

Hearing Aids and Surgeries

Hanna's deafness was always a trial to her. She wore a hearing aid, at first a rather primitive one with a rubber tube connecting a mouthpiece and an ear piece. As new hearing systems were developed, she found them less burdensome but costly. Anton liked his cigars, pipes and tobacco. Every time he spent money on his "vice" he gave Hanna an equal amount, which she carefully set aside for the next hearing aid. For their second furlough in 1930, Anton suggested they go by way of Europe. He had heard of a famous hearing specialist in Zurich. There they found a cheap hotel. Anton inquired at the desk about Dr. Nager and learned his fee was 75 francs. He did not have that much money and sadly remarked that his wife would have to get along without an examination. To add to his woes, Hanna was ill during most of the trip. One day he had just done laundry when there was a knock at the hotel door. An old man with a long beard asked, "May I come in?" Anton hesitated because wash was hanging around to dry and some was soaking in the basin, but courtesy won out; before long he began to tell his guest his problems. Suddenly, with tears in his eyes, the old man pressed an envelope into Anton's hand and left. It contained exactly 75 francs. In spite of his efforts, Anton never saw the man again. Hanna was examined by Dr. Nager, who thought he could help her preserve her present hearing and reduce the "head noises" that troubled her so much.

Since her latest pregnancy, two years previous, Hanna had not felt well. She had back and abdominal pain and frequent vaginal bleeding. When she went to the doctor in St. Louis he advised an immediate hysterectomy, telling Anton that she had been experiencing a great deal more pain than she admitted. Later in their furlough she had gall bladder surgery. Mathilda was asked to take a year away from school to help her mother and care for her two-year old brother Don, whom she had just met for the first time. The trip back to India was postponed a few months to allow time for Hanna to recover more fully.

Back in India

Once more there was a difficult and agonizing problem. It was obvious that living with complete strangers had not been a happy experience for Lydia and Mathilda, and Hanna insisted that, with two boys joining them, the American contingent of the family must stick together. She had decided to stay on in St. Louis, but at the last minute Pastor and Mrs. John Harms, who had returned from India because of his bad health, volunteered to welcome the young Lutzes into their large Nebraska farm parsonage and to be their legal guardians. The girls and Arnold went to Lutheran boarding high school and colleges in Nebraska and Kansas, while Erwin enrolled in eighth grade at Lyons, Nebraska. Once more Hanna went back to India with Anton.

Anton continued his seminary teaching. In 1938 he was named president of the school. In 1939 the St. Louis seminary awarded him a doctorate. Always a humble man, Anton was stunned and could not believe this undeserved honor. Hanna quietly assured him he had earned every bit of it.

The Lutz family in 1938
Back: Mildred, Arnold, Mathilda, Erwin, Lydia, Walter
Front: Don, Hanna, Anton, Edward

By this time the children were becoming self-sufficient. Lydia had found a sweetheart and was ready to settle down on a Nebraska farm. The boys worked on harvest crews in the summer and Erwin thought he would become a farmer (he changed his mind and went into teaching). Hanna was pleased that the family kept in touch and tried to spend vacations together, sometimes in a mission house in St. Louis.

World War II

As World War II expanded and the Japanese armies continued their relentless march as far as Burma, rumors flew that India was to be invaded next. Some of the missionaries panicked. The Mission Board gave permission for wives and children to return to the United States. Hanna and Anton felt safe in Nagercoil, but there was another problem. Their second-youngest son, Edward, had stayed in India for his early high school years; in two more years he would be 18 and subject to draft in the British army since he had been born on British soil. In spite of dangers on the high seas, it was decided that Edward and 13-year-old Don should leave India. It was a perilous journey; crossing the Atlantic the ship kept black shades over the portholes and issued life jackets as the captain charted a zig-zag course to avoid detection by German U-boats. Anton and Hanna kept their ears glued to the wireless radio for the daily reports of which ships had been sunk. And they prayed. A friend said they both aged ten years waiting for the telegram that the boys had arrived in New York safely.

Professor's Wife

Anton translated seminary textbooks into Tamil. He was a consultant to the Bible Society of India, Pakistan and Ceylon for a new Tamil translation of the Scriptures. He disciplined his students and dealt with other problems that arose. His experience and advice were sought by the Mission Board and novice missionaries. Wrote one: "One of the catechumens has two wives. He wants to be baptized and realizes he should leave one wife go, but does not know which. The women are sisters; he married the second because the first bore him no children. Now he has children from both wives."

Hanna's hearing improvement was short-lived. Once back in India the din in her ears became worse. The batteries in her new acousticon wore out, and it was hard to find replacements. As wife of the seminary president, she was frequently hostess to visiting dignitaries, to other missionaries and to students. Many years later an Indian pastor told her son Arnold that Hanna had given him milk and other food daily so he could continue at the seminary. Newly-arrived, frightened young missionary wives found her quiet graciousness reassuring, and they often sought her sensible advice.

The Final Homecoming

In 1946 Anton requested an early furlough. He was not feeling well but was sure that after a good rest he could return to his duties in India. On board the ship he suddenly could not walk, and he arrived at St. Louis in a lot of pain. The doctor withheld the facts; Anton was told he had a severe kind of arthritis, and his medication brought temporary relief. But the pain returned and finally Anton realized he had terminal cancer. He would not return to India. His last days in Lutheran Hospital were very painful; Hanna faithfully kept a bedside vigil. She had just turned her back to prepare his luncheon tray when he stopped breathing. After 33-1/2 years Hanna came full circle. She was back in St. Louis to stay.

In anticipation of his parents' furlough and to have a place where the family could congregate, Arnold had instigated the purchase of a house in St. Louis. Mathilda, Erwin and Mildred had teaching jobs in the city. Walter and Edward were at the seminary, so Hanna was not alone. But she was lonely. The children were occupied with their own lives. She had been in India for so long that "home" was strange and unfamiliar, and she felt she really didn't belong anywhere. She missed Anton acutely. Hanna lived two more years before dying of a brain aneurism.

Eulogy

In India the chapel at Thirumangulam is dedicated to the memory of Anton Lutz. Hanna's only tribute is a document in the files at the Concordia Historical Institute in St. Louis, specifying "Mrs. Johanna Lutz is a duly called and salaried evangelical missionary in the employ of the Evangelical Lutheran Church of Missouri, Ohio and Other States." Hanna would have laughed at the word "salaried," and she would have been the first to deny that she was a missionary. But she was.

Elizabeth — 1995

"Yes she was!" echoes Elizabeth. "I do think she was a missionary. I had never heard much about my great-grandmother, so the story was all new to me. I didn't know she was hard-of-hearing. She sounds like a really brave person — if I were half-deaf, I don't know if I could go to a country where I didn't know anybody at all. Maybe that's why my grandpa went into deaf work.

"My great-grandmother was a missionary by the way she helped the people who always came and sat on her porch. Just supporting her husband was a great help; without her my great-grandfather could not have done half of the things he did.

"My grandmother, Juanita Lutz, was also a missionary. When we lived in India we'd visit our grandparents for Christmas, and they'd come to Kodaikanal for vacations. When my sister Jessica was born, my grandma came and stayed with my mother and helped her for a while. She'd always do things with me. I remember there was a big lake, about three miles around. I got a bunch of people to sign a paper; they'd give money to some charity we were collecting for at school if I walked around the lake. Mom didn't have time to walk around with me, and I was too little to do it by myself. So grandma got out there and walked around the lake with me. At that time I never thought of her as a great missionary. She was just my grandma."

*Juanita Becker before her
marriage to Arnold Lutz*

II. Juanita

When Juanita Becker told her father she wanted to marry Arnold Lutz, her father said, "But what will you do if he returns to India?" "Why," she replied, "I will go with him." Nita had mixed feelings about that possibility. Arnold had told her many stories about growing up in South India, and memory had painted them so romantically she could hardly wait to see that beautiful, exotic land. But she wasn't quite sure she wanted to live there.

Arnold indeed planned to follow in his father's footsteps, and in 1942 he accepted an assignment from the LCMS Mission Board to be a missionary in India. But World War II was still raging, so he went instead to South Dakota and a year later to Minneapolis to work among the deaf. During his high school years Arnold had a bad ear infection that left him temporarily deaf. He remembered his mother's frustration and limitations with deafness and decided to learn sign language. Even though Arnold recovered his hearing, he never lost his empathy for the hearing impaired. He could not look into the future to see how the Lord would bring deaf missions to India through him.

Arnold and Nita married in 1944. Nita loved to hear Arnold and his siblings reminisce about India when they came to Minneapolis for summer vacations and holidays. Two years later the Mission Board again approached Arnold about going to India. He accepted, and Nita was quite willing to go.

Journey to India

So soon after the war getting across the Pacific and into India was an exercise in frustration and in waiting for visas, permits and ship passage. Meanwhile Arnold's parents arrived in the United States, and Nita met her in-laws for the first time. She had six weeks to get acquainted and to learn India-style housekeeping from Hanna. When a maritime strike finally ended in mid-December 1946, Arnold and Nita boarded a converted troop ship bound for India. With responsibility for their two young sons, Nita was assigned to a separate women's cabin with 12 other women. Already she was learning that the realities of life as a missionary were not as romantic and exciting as memories.

Even though there were two other missionary families traveling with them, there was no one to meet the ship when they landed in Madras a month later. Arnold had to find a way to their destination in Nagercoil, partly by train, partly by a rented automobile that jolted over rough roads. By the end of the long ordeal, Nita had regained her adventuresome spirit, and she and her year-old son gleefully identified the bullocks, cows, goats and occasional elephants sharing the road with them. She gasped with delight at the beauty of the sunset behind the waving palm trees.

It was dark when the family arrived at the Nagercoil mission compound, and still they found no one to greet them. Finally missionary wife Agnes Landgraf came out of one of the houses. When they hailed her, she welcomed them joyously but wondered where the hosts who had driven to meet them were. Two flat tires and a different route had caused them to miss each other. Now the welcome was most cordial. Nita and Arnold spent several weeks getting acquainted with the missionaries in Nagercoil. Everyone was anxious to hear the latest news about Arnold's parents and was concerned Anton was so ill.

The first task of a newly arrived missionary is to learn the language. Nita had learned a few phrases of Tamil from Arnold, but he had been away from India so long he had forgotten much. After their brief visit in Nagercoil, Nita and Arnold repacked for a three-month stay in Kodaikanal, where they would both be tutored by a *munshi.*

The boarding school at Kodaikanal was without houseparents; Nita and Arnold were asked to fill in temporarily. Instead of two children, Nita suddenly had 25 boys and girls, ages six to 18. She found herself doctoring bruised knees and elbows, dosing coughs and colds, wiping away tears of homesickness and seeing that the children were bundled up for the mountain winter. Her adaptability was taxed to its limits when the anticipated few months extended to a year-and-a-half. She had brought only a few suitcases and was not prepared for the colder mountain temperatures. Finding time for language study was a problem, and Nita found Tamil difficult to learn. It is an old tongue with many words and nuances of meaning; it has been labeled one of the most difficult in the world, next to Arabic.

The school at Kodaikanal with the church in the background

In Hanna's Footsteps

When Arnold and Nita finally moved to the mission compound in Vadakangulam, they lived in the same bungalow that Anton had designed and built for Hanna. The Vadakangulam Lutheran Church had become a large and thriving congregation. There was an elementary and high school and a boys' boarding hostel, with a girls' hostel to be added. Missionaries Pastor Henry Peckman and principal W. C. Dukewitz, a bachelor, shared a newer bungalow on the Vadakangulam compound. When Betty Rose Wulf arrived to teach in the high school, she lived with Arnold and Nita. The first room in the house was hers; then came a guest room and a communal living/dining room. Even though the rooms were large and spacious, that left only two for the Lutz family, out of which they had to carve a study for Arnold.

Nita settled down to a life very much like that of her mother-in-law — she even inherited Hanna's furniture. She also had eight children, three of them delivered by the same doctor who had tended Hanna. There were the same number of servants: cook, gardener and *ayah*. Nita felt fortunate that she was able to employ people who were experienced; her only servant problem was to make them understand that the children should have regular chores and should learn responsibility. Nita learned to sift the weevils out of flour and to bake her own bread. Her visions of exotic experiences were often lost in the daily humdrum of mothering and supervising a household. It was fascinating to watch the darting transparent lizards scamper up the bungalow walls, the flies they had just swallowed painfully visible, but when white ants found a crack in the cement floor and built a foot-high mound overnight, she despaired of ever winning the constant battle against their forays.

But Nita was not Hanna, and it was a generation later. Tropical diseases and infections were still virulent, but antibiotics were readily available. The children went barefoot or wore sandals. "It's easier to wash feet than to clean shoes," reasoned Nita. And they were allowed to play in the sun without *topees*. "After all, it's the same sun here as in the United States."

Improvements and Changes

A generator provided electricity for several hours each evening, and there was a kerosene-operated refrigerator. The bathroom held a large concrete basin from which one could fill the wash bowl or "flush" the toilet with a bucketful. Taking a shower meant standing over the drain in the concrete floor and pouring buckets of sun-warmed water over the body. In time electricity and indoor plumbing were installed.

Independence came to India a year after Nita and Arnold arrived. In the small village of Vadakangulam it brought few immediate changes. Instead of being first to be waited on in markets, post offices and government offices, Europeans had to stand in line with everyone else. But the missionaries had not demanded these privileges anyway. Since very few Indian women went shopping or conducted the family business, Nita found she could stand in the women's line and get waited on long before Arnold in the men's line inched forward. Many English officials left India and businesses were taken over by Indians; some canned meats and delicacies were in short supply.

More far-reaching changes came with the new government's "India for the Indians" policy. Forgetting that Christianity in India dated back even farther than in the western world, many of the new leaders saw the white missionaries and the songs, liturgies and church organization they brought as foreign. As long as they kept their visas up-to-date those already living in India could stay, but few new missionaries could be added. The church had to rely more and more on its Indian pastors, teachers and leaders. In 1958 the India Evangelical Lutheran Church became a separate entity and, a year later, a partner church of the LCMS.

Missionary Wife

Arnold was a missionary-evangelist and also managed the area mission schools. He preached every Sunday and in between as well, but he did not have a call to any specific congregation. He particularly enjoyed going to the villages in the evening. Taking along a teacher or group of boarding school boys, he would hang a lantern on a tree branch and soon a crowd would gather. Sometimes the boys sang, often he showed a filmstrip. Once when a slide showing a painting of Christ appeared on the screen, an old woman exclaimed, "What a beautiful *swami* the Christians have! What fools we are to do *puja* [homage] to such ugly old *swami!*" It was a great joy when an individual or family responded to the Gospel and came forward for baptism.

Often Arnold was gone for days at a time, but when the distance was shorter Nita and a child or two went along. The people would wait until Arnold arrived to pour out of their huts and accompany him to the *pandel* church, a shelter with mud walls several feet high and a palm leaf roof. The dirt floor was sealed with cow dung, and the audience squatted on grass mats, the women on one side, the men on the other. The only furniture was a table for an altar and a chair for the visiting preacher. As she looked at the swaying palm trees beyond the low walls, Nita felt close to God; she loved to hear the congregation sing hymns in Tamil. It was a bit disturbing when the Indian men and women, who had a habit of chewing betel, would get up and spit the red saliva over the wall, or when tired children wandered at will. Nita found herself staring at the elongated ears of some of the women and learned it was from wearing heavy earrings. It was a mark of wealth to wear jewels — wrist and ankle bangles; finger, toe, ear and nose rings; necklaces. When they became Christians many women gave up this ostentation.

Instead of a motorcycle, Arnold was assigned a car — a Model B Ford. After World War II gas was rationed. The nearest petrol station was in Nagercoil; whoever drove to town bought the meager ration and stored it in gas cans to be doled out as needed. Cars did not hold up long on the rough, dirt roads; wire, hair-pins and even cow dung were used for temporary repairs. Flat tires were common. Once when Nita went part way on one of Arnold's mission rounds, intending to spend a few days with another missionary family, there were two flat tires. Since it was late afternoon, Nita proceeded by bus while Arnold stayed to repair the tires. The women's side of the bus was packed, but Nita felt her two little boys warranted her a place in the men's section, much to the irritation of the man in the adjoining seat.

Every Monday the Vadakangulam missionaries would pile into the car and drive to Nagercoil for an English worship service. Over the rough, potholed roads filled with pedestrians, bullock carts, cows and goats, it took an hour to drive the 12 miles. They would enjoy tea at a fellow missionary's home and after the 5:00 p.m. service would return for a meal and fellowship. Several hours later, after bidding farewell to their hosts, they would stop at the markets to shop, and if a trip to the doctor was warranted, he would be in his office until about 10:00 p.m. They finally arrived home around midnight.

Nita came to appreciate the hospitality and fellowship of the other missionaries. So far from their relatives, the American minority took the place of family; there was a common bond with Christian missionaries, businessmen and travelers. Although their personalities were very different, she and Kay Peckman spent a good deal of time together and became good friends. Wishing to return the hospitality of their city hosts, Nita and Kay invited them all to "come to the country" for Christmas. This soon became an annual tradition.

In most cases the missionaries' wives were as committed as their husbands to bringing the Gospel to the Indian people. They were not paid for their services, but the Mission Board expected them to volunteer as needs arose. Some filled in as teachers or supervised the girls' boarding schools; others taught women sewing, embroidery or crocheting. In the Ambur district those who were nurses helped with Bethesda Lutheran Hospital's roadside dispensaries, and most administered basic first aid from their bungalow verandas. Nita found her niche in her secretarial skills. She typed Arnold's sermons, reports and letters and helped with financial records. For a while she was the fiscal officer for Missouri Evangelical Lutheran India Mission (MELIM), the organization of the missionaries in India.

Difficulties and Opposition

The Peckmans did not return after their 1952 furlough, and an Indian pastor came to serve the Vadakangulam congregation. In spite of their growing numbers, the Christians were still a small minority and faced many problems. Friendships developed between the castes at the seminary, but once the men became pastors of congregations it was difficult to breach the old exclusions. And there was persecution. Especially in the small villages the men could lose their jobs. Already living in poverty and debt, some were afraid to openly confess Christ. One night Nita and Arnold heard a lot of shouting and chanting and beating of sticks across the road. The Hindu relatives of a teacher's wife were exorcising the demon that had caused her to leave her family and their idols.

Polly Buehner, a missionary wife in nearby Trivandrum told a much sadder story. One day the Hindu relatives of a teacher's wife nagged and maligned and shouted at the young girl so long that she put on all her beautiful saris, one over the other, and either she or someone else set them on fire. No one knew who was responsible. Polly was sure the Lord gave her the strength and will to grab a flashlight and hurry through the dark rice fields to the London Mission hospital more than a mile away. There she knelt before the small figure stretched out on the floor, her body covered with banana leaves turned black from the burns. Polly began to recite the Lord's prayer in Malalayam, the language of that area. Soon she saw the girl's lips moving; her eyes opened wide and she said, "Jesus is coming for me!" The funeral just before midnight (burial in India was always the same day) gave Missionary Andrew Buehner, who had been away from home all that day, a wonderful opportunity for sharing the Gospel with both the Hindu and Christian mourners.

Traveling Days

A rnold's responsibilities stretched to the supervision of more distant congregations, so after 18 years at Vadakangulam he moved his family to the city of Madurai, a Brahmin area. Not wishing to offend their vegetarian neighbors, their faithful cook would take the bus to purchase the daily food supplies, piling vegetables atop his basket to hide the meat. When it was not needed for the mission, Nita would drive the car to the markets; she loved talking to the merchants and poking around in the bazaars, and she was never afraid to go there alone. She was sure the Lord was protecting her, because only once did she have a flat tire and that was in an area where help was accessible.

When the children were all in boarding school, Nita decided to travel with Arnold. They had the use of a Jeep station wagon and needed all the room for camping equipment, cooking supplies, and books and files. When possible they stayed the night at government tourist bungalows; often they spread their sleeping bags on the hard wooden benches of a church or school. They brought with them large containers of water

Arnold and Nita Lutz with their children in 1959

(drinking their own boiled water was the most important strategy for staying healthy); a Primus stove; cans of sardines, corned beef, baked beans, rice, bread, peanut butter and jam; a bucket and basin for washing; a first-aid kit; and plenty of mosquito repellent. Vegetables and fruit were purchased along the way.

In time there were more local restaurants, and they began patronizing the ones run by Brahmins who have rituals for cleanliness. Any hot drink (coffee, tea, even milk) was served at the boiling point and was safe to order. Meals were served on fresh banana leaves, and food was eaten with the right hand in Indian fashion. Nita and Arnold looked forward to a good Indian meal and decided the spices kept them healthier and made them feel better in the tropical heat. Finally they took along only some instant coffee or tea, cookies and a jar of jelly or peanut butter. Eating in a restaurant was simpler and cheaper.

As they made the rounds of the various villages, Nita visited the women while Arnold talked to the men. She usually wore a sari, finding it more suitable and modest for sitting on the floor, and she learned to be quite comfortable squatting cross-legged on a woven palm mat. Sometimes stools would be provided for the visitors and would be carried from house to house as they made the rounds. Indian women are very hospitable; Nita and Arnold had to be careful of causing offense by overlooking one of the small one-room mud huts. They were always offered a drink and a snack. Nita preferred coffee, tea or tender coconut water to a "color," a sweet carbonated drink she knew was not always germ-free. She was not offended by the personal questions the women often asked, because she knew they did not consider them rude. The Indians accepted that westerners had different ways than theirs, and she could return that courtesy. For example, the Indians thought it was very unsanitary that the Europeans cleaned their teeth with brushes that were used over and over — the Indians used, and discarded, tree branches or charcoal dust.

Before leaving each home Arnold would have a brief devotion and everyone would kneel for a prayer and blessing.

Prayer played a vital part in the life of Indian Christians. Frequently they would gather at a home for a *viddarathanal* (home service). A lyric would be sung, a Psalm read, and the leader prayed, emphasizing the special needs of the sick and of the congregation.

Beginning Deaf Work in India

Back in 1917 Arnold's father had suggested the Mission Board start work among the blind and deaf, reporting that he was ministering to seven blind and three deaf people in the Nagercoil area. For 20 years Arnold searched for a way of reaching India's hearing impaired. In 1970 he found a Christian instructor at a school in Ambur who was willing to train several young Lutheran teachers to work with the deaf. In 1980 Indian Pastor Christudoss dedicated his ministry to deaf work. Arnold developed finger spelling for the Tamil language and published a book of signs for teachers. Nita patiently typed and retyped his manuscripts for final printing.

Retirement Days

Back in the United States after his retirement in 1981, Arnold felt restless. He knew there was still much he could do for the deaf in India, so he offered to go back as a volunteer. He and Nita rented a small Indian bungalow in Madras. Knowing they would be on the road two or three weeks each month, and with electricity, refrigeration and ceiling fans now available, Nita decided to keep house without the aid of servants. Her morning exercise was a walk to the market; in the evening she might take another walk to have wheat ground at the mill — though the car was available when she needed it. The Mission Board paid their travel, and she and Arnold lived quite comfortably on social security.

In 1988 Nita and Arnold finally returned to the United States to stay. They bought a home in Ames, Iowa, near their third son Tim. Three years later history repeated itself when Arnold, like his father, developed cancer. Juanita realized how times had changed when her son Steve, a missionary doctor in Papua New Guinea, flew home to be with his father during his last days. When Anton died 44 years earlier, Arnold had just arrived in India and there was no way he could have made the month-long sea journey to visit his dying father. Juanita continues to live in their Iowa home. The deaf work in India remains dear to her heart.

Elizabeth — 1995

"My grandma helped the mission a lot," muses Elizabeth, "the way she did all my grandpa's typing and went with him everywhere. In my grandmother's and great-grandmother's time, most women were housewives — yes, there were nurses and teachers and secretaries too.

"Now women are doing a lot more things. I think women can get in there and do almost anything. There are a lot of volunteer opportunities with the Lutheran mission where you can go over and help, like setting up air strips in Papua New Guinea. Anyone can do that. When my parents went to Kodaikanal to be houseparents, my mom and dad were both commissioned for the work. There was a special service for them at the church in Springfield, Missouri, where we were living then, and a mission executive came from St. Louis to commission them.

"My parents, Gary and Alice Paul, were both missionaries, but neither one of them was an ordained minister."

III. Alice

Alice Lutz's marriage to Gary Paul at Our Redeemer Lutheran Church in South St. Louis created quite a stir in the conservative German community. Alice wore a gold-bordered white sari; her bridesmaids wore pale green saris; her mother and sisters-in-law, as well as a number of other female guests, wore saris

Alice Lutz in her wedding sari

of many hues, creating a beautiful rainbow of these graceful dresses of India.

One Little Girl

Growing up in India, Nita's and Arnold's only girl among seven brothers, Alice sometimes felt sorry for herself. At about age six she was old enough to realize her mother was going to have another baby, and she began praying for a sister. She already had four older brothers and one younger and desperately wanted a female playmate. Every night she prayed. When the new baby was another boy, she was very disappointed. It took about a week for her to decide that baby boys were fun too.

Sometimes Alice would go to the boarding school across the street from her parents' bungalow in Vadakangulam, and the high school girls would teach her Indian dances or show her how to drape the half-saris that they wore when they reached puberty. But most of the time she was outdoors in the sandpile playing cars and trucks with her brothers. Sometimes they gave her a hard time, and she would come in and complain to her mother — the boys did this or the boys did that — but it was important to her to do what her brothers did.

Nita's veranda medical dispensary made a deep impression on Alice. Once a man came in a panic. He was picking up bricks, and as he put one against himself a snake bit him. Nita gave him a liquid medicine; he walked around for a while and returned for another spoonful. The treatment continued for some time, and all the while the man was moaning that he was going to die. Whether the man really was bitten by a snake or what the medicine was, Alice did not know, but he did recover. After this dramatic incident, Alice decided she would become a nurse.

Since she was the only girl in her family, people were always giving Alice dolls. She seldom played with them because she was quite happy with her brothers' toys. When she was about ten years old, her parents cleared a storeroom in the bungalow so she could have her own room. Then she began lining up her dolls along the wall — one would have a fever, one a sore leg, one a cast on the arm, one a headache, and one would be her baby. Once a week she treated her patients.

Alice trying on a sari

Thanks to her mother comparing it to a grand adventure and her brothers already there, Alice was excited about going to the Lutheran boarding school at Kodaikanal. Nita and Arnold always drove the children into the hills and up the narrow road, so Alice never felt alone or abandoned. There were two teachers at the school, with about 30 to 40 children boarding there, some of them attending the interdenominational high school across the street. Most of her classmates were missionaries' children Alice already knew. Instead of six in the entire school, as there had been during her father's school days, there were that many in her class; and her high school graduating class numbered 36. Nor did Alice have any trauma after high school when she came to St. Louis, Missouri, to begin nurses' training at Lutheran Hospital — once more her older brothers had preceded her and were there when she needed comfort or advice.

Back to India

Alice's memories of India were good ones, and she wanted Gary to see that beautiful country. In 1975, about a year-and-a-half after their marriage, they scraped together enough money and flew to Madurai to visit Nita and Arnold. They spent a night in Madras. As the taxi drove through the streets to their hotel, Gary saw the dirt and filth, the people sleeping in the streets. This was not the India his wife had painted so nostalgically. He was ready to turn around and head back to America!

But after several weeks with his in-laws and meeting the people they worked with, the spell of India had won him. When it was time to return home he suggested, tongue-in-cheek, that Alice send a telegram to the hospital where she was working saying they couldn't get a flight so they would have to stay a few weeks longer.

Back home in the United States Gary and Alice talked of going to live in India and wrote to the Lutheran boarding school at Kodaikanal to see if there was an opening for houseparents. There was no response. Five years and two children later, they decided it was time for Elizabeth and Erich to meet their maternal grandparents. They again flew to India for a visit and discovered there was going to be a vacancy at the Kodaikanal boarding school. When they returned to the United States, they applied to the LCMS Department of Missions. When Gary told his parents what they had done, their first reaction was "You must be crazy!" But less than a year later Alice and Gary had been commissioned as missionary-houseparents and were on their way back to India.

Houseparents

Changes at the Kodaikanal school had come rapidly. With a dwindling number of Lutheran missionaries remaining in India, the Lutheran school had been closed; it made more sense economically for the church to supply a teacher for the school across the street and to share classrooms. The Kodaikanal inter-denominational school had become an international school. It was distinguished from other boarding schools in that its curriculum remained American rather than British. Teachers came from all over the world but most were Indian. Many of the pupils were Indians who had grown up in other countries; some were U.S. citizens whose parents wanted them exposed to the country of their origin. At one time there were seven different nationalities among the 25 to 30 children at the Lutheran boarding home. Supervising this mix was a challenge for the houseparents. No longer were they one family, bonded by all being missionaries' children. Many of the students came from wealthy business families and had a lot of spending money.

Alice was in charge of planning the meals, purchasing food, and supervising the three cooks, two laundresses and two cleaning ladies. She nursed and as best she could mothered the boarding school children. Gary did all of the bookkeeping and banking and managed the property, including the vacation cottages that were rented and eventually sold. The property had been transferred to the India Evangelical Lutheran Church. The fees paid by the students adequately covered running and operating the boarding home. Alice and Gary reported to MELIM, but their salary came from the Mission Board in the United States. Back in 1928, the Mission Board had explained its policy this way: "The status of wives of our missionaries is that they are not only wives and mothers, but that they are missionaries. Their salary is included in the salary of the husband." It was an adequate salary for India; Gary and Alice were able to do some traveling and collect a small nest-egg for their return to the United States. "But when we had to buy a house and two cars and furniture in the United States, that nest-egg didn't last long," says Alice ruefully. "It takes two salaries to make it here!"

At the end of their first three-year term there was a three-month furlough. Gary's parents had a chance to meet their newest granddaughter, Jessica. Then the family went back to India for another stint. By that time there was only one missionary child left in the international school, and the Lutheran property was to be converted to a boys' dormitory. In 1987 Alice and Gary decided to leave India. They spent another three years as houseparents at the Bible Translators Institute of Linguistics in Papua New Guinea. The family returned to live in the United States in 1990.

Gary and Alice Paul with infant Jessica, Erich and Elizabeth

India Today

"The India I knew as a child is not the same India I returned to," says Alice. "And I'm sure India today is quite different than when we left it. Changes have come very rapidly — I think even faster than in the United States, because India had farther to come into the 20th century. Yet in the villages the old traditions, customs and superstitions persist. The poor people are still extremely poor."

Since independence from British rule in 1948, India has survived as a democracy. There are now 167 Indian-born pastors in the India Evangelical Lutheran Church; the seminary graduates about 30 students each year. Some districts are 50 percent Christian — there are 27 million Christians in India. But that's only 3 percent of the total population, 900 million people. It's predicted that by the year 2005 India's population will surpass that of China!

Compared to the millions of people in India — Hindus, Muslims, Sikhs, Buddhists, Jains, Parsees, Animists — the Christians are like a few grains of sand on an ocean beach. But they have been firmly established and form a vibrant nucleus for the spread of the Gospel in the twentieth-first century.

Elizabeth — 1995

Elizabeth Paul, 1995

"**A**nd now we're back in the United States," concludes Elizabeth. "That's good too. I didn't remember America before I came back, so it's been a big adventure, like going to a new country and meeting new people. When my parents moved to Papua New Guinea, we lived in a community where about 700 American expatriates were living, so I knew how to react to Americans when we got to the States. I don't have any problems making friends, but I had more trouble fitting in here than I had any other place. I don't know why. Americans think they are the greatest and no other country is as good as America. But I've lived in other countries, and I think they're just as good. And I really can't understand the prejudice here. I was brought up in places where most people were not my skin color or my religion. I get into big discussions about it with a lot of my friends, and I think it's really exciting because they'll look at it from my point of view and say, 'Yeah, we are kind of self-centered.'

"Living in India has made our family an international one. My uncle is a medical missionary in Papua New Guinea. He lives up in the mountains where it's undeveloped and there are still tribes who have never seen white people. One of my cousins is half Vietnamese; she and I both want to work overseas.

"I want to go into international service at college this fall. What do I want to do with that? I would work in community development, like the Peace Corps does. I'd like to go to different countries, into a village or community and find out what they think they need help with — like if they need a more effective way of getting water or help with their agriculture or whatever. Then I'd help them get the things they need and help them set them up and learn how to use them. I'd love to go back to India and Papua New Guinea.

"Sharing my faith in Jesus plays into my career choice. In India, for instance, they're restricting entry for new missionaries. You really can't be a missionary there in the old way. The bulk of mission work will be done by Indians themselves and by teachers and people in community development, like nurse Alice Brauer and her program with women and children. In working with development agencies and government programs, there will be more opportunities to get through closed borders. It would be nice to go to a village that hasn't been reached by missionaries. I can tell the people what I believe, then I can be a missionary too!"

Louise Mueller has written devotions for Portals of Prayer, *Bible studies for the LWML and is former editor-in-chief of the* Lutheran Woman's Quarterly. *She has three adult children and lives in St. Louis, Missouri, with her husband Howard.*

Angela
of Mercy

by Louise Mueller

Prologue

Cora Doermann was a brave woman. It took courage to leave her family in the United States soon after World War I and undertake the long sea journey to India with her missionary husband Carl. And in spring 1922 when the time for her first child's birth was near, Cora boarded a train and traveled alone the 50 miles from Thirupati to Ambur so the newly arrived American Lutheran doctor, Theodore Doederlein, could deliver her baby. "She must have been a little frightened when the birth finally occurred and the doctor was 40 miles away at a clinic in Krishnigiri," muses Ellen Hillmer. "Nurse Angela Rehwinkel took charge. I guess I'll never know just how much the first-time mother and the novice nurse supported each other."

"I was that baby," Ellen continues. "Years later I learned I was the first missionary child Angela delivered. I was by no means the last!"

For 37-1/2 years Angela Rehwinkel was the nursing superintendent of Bethesda Lutheran Hospital in Ambur, South India. For more than 30 of those years, it was her faithfulness and tenacity that kept the hospital alive. For the countless women and men who were her patients during those years, Angela was indeed an angel of mercy.

I. Beginnings

"But they're so ugly!" Angela wailed, looking down at the sturdy, scuffed shoes encasing her small feet. "Little girls don't wear boys' shoes!" Her sobs and protests were to no avail. In the cold Wisconsin winter she could hardly go to school barefoot, and for a poor minister's family at the turn of the century, hand-me-downs were the rule. Angela Rehwinkel hated wearing her older brothers' shoes, and she vowed that when she grew up she would have only pretty ladies' shoes — a whole closet full of them!

After her grade-school education was completed, Angela did housework for a family in Horicon, Wisconsin; they encouraged her dream of becoming a nurse and gave financial help. She graduated from St. John Lutheran Hospital, Red Wing, Minnesota, studied at University Hospital, Minneapolis, and was the superintendent and administrator of Sartori Memorial Hospital in Cedar Falls, Iowa. Her brother Alfred, a student at Concordia Seminary in St. Louis,

Angela Rehwinkel's graduation from nursing school

Missouri, encouraged her interest in foreign missions and arranged for her to meet Dr. Frederick Brand, Mission Director for The Lutheran Church—Missouri Synod. In 1920 Angela volunteered to serve as a missionary nurse in India.

Angela never forgot her childhood resolution. She loved pretty clothes; on her travels she purchased beautiful Indian saris and Philippine dresses in a rainbow of colors, as well as smart footwear. It was a facet of her personality her coworkers seldom saw since a nurse's uniform did not allow for frivolity. Yet coworkers remember that her white dress and cap were impeccably clean and starched, and her shoes were as neat and trim as comfort allowed.

In 1913 the American-based Lutheran Church—Missouri Synod (LCMS) resolved to initiate medical mission work in India, women's societies pledged $600 to the cause and Lula Ellermann began a veranda medical dispensary from her bungalow in Bargur, India. It was a small effort amidst overwhelming need, her fellow missionaries were not always supportive, and she often shut down the dispensary for weeks and months at a time to care for ill missionary personnel. In 1921 Dr. Theodore Doederlein took a leave of absence from his Chicago practice to found a hospital in Ambur, South India, a town of 20,000 in the heart of the area where the LCMS had begun its foreign mission effort some 25 years earlier. He treated patients in a tent while buildings were being constructed. At the end of the year, nurses Angela Rehwinkel and Etta Herold arrived.

Even by the standards of that time, Bethesda Lutheran Hospital had an unpretentious beginning. Three single-story bungalows, surrounded by spacious verandas and connected by covered walkways, housed treatment rooms for outpatients and a central compounding room (pharmacy). The verandas were the waiting rooms. Inpatients were housed in two eight-bed wards, one for men and one for women. There was no electricity; rooms were lit by kerosene lanterns. Windows were barred but not screened. A few sheds provided housing for the Indian staff. There were no quarters for American nurses.

Bethesda Hospital on its dedication day

The first resident patient was a woman with a gangrenous foot. As missionary Erwin Meinzen toured the new hospital with Dr. Doederlein, the stench and oozing puss were so nauseating he fainted, hitting his head on the metal bedstead. He became the second overnight patient. Thanks to the doctor's careful attention, Missionary Meinzen could deliver a brief English sermon at the formal dedication of Bethesda Lutheran Hospital the next day, January 14, 1923. Angela Rehwinkel, Etta Herold and Lula Ellermann worked with Dr. Doederlein until he returned to the United States in 1923. Before he left India, Dr. Doederlein hired an Indian doctor, nurse and compounder (pharmacist) and appointed Angela Rehwinkel nursing superintendent of the hospital.

The original intent was also to begin medical work at Krishnigiri, 40 miles west of Ambur. Whichever area proved better would be the permanent hospital site. In spite of lack of funds for building, the organization of India missionaries, Missouri Evangelical Lutheran India Mission (MELIM), decided to open a dispensary at Krishnigiri in 1922. Dr. Doederlein scheduled regular visits and Etta Herold was placed in charge. She nursed the wife and young daughter of missionary Pastor Emil Noffke, but they died of diphtheria within a few days of each other. A year later, in 1926, Etta and Emil Noffke were married. In 1927 Pastor Noffke accepted a call to Australia, his home country. That ended the Krishnigiri medical effort.

Etta had left, but the hospital at Ambur survived. Angela Rehwinkel stayed.

II. With Tortoise Steps

Angela had good sense, deep faith, compassion and a fine sense of humor. She adjusted remarkably well to India's tropical climate. "Now don't emigrate to Ambur to cool off," she wrote friends at home. "It's hot, hotter, hottest — sometimes 105°-106° in the shade." Angela could see beauty even in the pestering bugs attracted to her candle as she sat writing.

"I wish you could see the different varieties on my desk — big and small, beautiful and homely, silver, black, green, brown, spotted — the flying ants are the worst! The sun has just set, and it was so beautiful I forget about the heat and filth."

Angela's ability to accept and adjust to the realities of life in India and her tenacity kept the medical mission of the LCMS alive for more than 30 years. At times the task fell on her exclusively, and she had all she could do to keep the hospital going.

One of Angela's early purchases was a team of bullocks and a *vandi* (enclosed passenger cart), which she named "The Black Moriah." The bullocks' main job was to draw water from the hospital well into a small tank. Everyone connected with the hospital got their water from this tank by dipping in their buckets and pots. In 1933 an elevated water tank was built, and pipes were installed to bring the water (still drawn by the faithful bullocks) into several hospital rooms.

In 1931 Angela wrote, "I received your letter telling us that $155 has been sent for a new refrigerator. How we can get a refrigerator without electricity I do not know!" Missionary Paul Heckel brought out a small generator and offered to install two lights in the delivery room if the hospital would get the wires and posts. Full electricity came in 1938 with lights and outlets in each room. The funds for a refrigerator had been carefully saved; a used box with a new unit was purchased and installed in the ladies' bungalow where Angela prepared the food for patients needing special diets.

The hospital laundry had always been done by a *dhoby*, a washerman who took the soiled clothes to the riverside and pounded them clean on stones. With electric power available, Angela decided it was time to purchase a washing machine. The Mission Board told her to pick one from the Montgomery Ward catalog and it would be sent over with the next arriving missionary. Dr. Norbert Leckband, who was working at Bethesda at the time, thought Angela's choice far too small and inadequate. He wanted to include a complete laundry in his plan for a modern, expanded hospital. But he was so busy with the mobile dispensary (and he did not like to write letters anyway) that his suggestions did not reach the Mission Board. In her quiet way, Angela simply set up the machine in the yard and put it to work. It did wear out and had to be replaced with a larger one, but meantime the hospital linens were clean.

In 1942 a maternity wing and nurses' residence were added with a $5,000 gift from the Northern Illinois Women's Missionary Society. Angela's friend, Missionary Meinert Grumm, who was an active member of the hospital board, designed the buildings. When the Mission Board in the United States became alarmed by the spread of World War II and instructed a postponement, Pastor Grumm "mislaid" the letter until it was too late to halt construction.

Not all the other missionaries agreed with Dr. Doederlein that "medical mission work relieves suffering, both spiritual as well as physical, and is a demonstration of the fruit of faith — love for our fellow man," and when money was scarce some suggested closing the hospital. Fortunately the Mission Board did not agree.

Equipment wore out, rubber items deteriorated and rotted. "So many years without a real doctor and everything and everybody has gotten in such a rut. Many things are used up," Angela moaned. "One learns by experience to do without all the modern hospital equipment." In spite of the difficulties and primitive conditions, Bethesda Hospital survived and grew. In 1929 Angela reported, "The hospital cared for 7,586 dispensary patients during the past year." By 1931 another nurse and a night watchman had been added to the staff. The number of infant deliveries each year rose from 20 in the early 1920s to 600 in 1953. In 1938 22,474 patients were treated at Bethesda. Wrote Missionary Grumm: "The one constant factor through all these changes and vicissitudes has been our superintendent, Angela Rehwinkel ... Bethesda Hospital and Miss

Rehwinkel are so much identified that it is hard for us to think of the two separately."

III. Sickness, Superstition and Healing

The first trial Angela faced was to see so many people around her who needed help and be unable to give it. "Anyone who has not lived in a country where modern medical aid reaches only 20 percent of the people cannot realize the extent of human suffering and misery prevalent in all parts of India," Angela wrote. The caste system, initiated by the Brahmins who had conquered India many centuries earlier, separated the people into rigid social groups. Most of them lived in small villages. One-sixth of the population were *pariahs* (outcasts), the poorest of the poor, who were not permitted to draw water from the village well lest it be contaminated. Instead they used germ-infested ditches and puddles. There was no medical care in the villages. Disease was rampant; superstition and apathetic acceptance of *karma* ("what the gods write on our foreheads") aggravated the suffering. Animism (god-spirits in nature who had to be placated) dated back to the Dravidians, India's earliest inhabitants. Placating the village gods, whose chief function was inflicting or warding off disease, took precedence over the worship of Brahma, Siva and Vishnu, the Hindu gods.

Charms, ritual and reciting of sacred verses were the treatments for epidemics and diseases. When a sickly baby was born, it was branded on the abdomen, wrists and ankles. The wounds often became infected and the infant died. Sore eyes were treated with an emulsion of red pepper, causing great pain and often blindness. Fever patients were confined to their small airless huts and were not washed or given water until they recuperated (if they did!). On the other hand, women in labor were placed outdoors in the hot sun, because it was bad luck to give birth in the house. If a woman's first baby died, it was buried under the dirt floor of the veranda for a week, after which the body was thrown into a pit. Superstition said that without this procedure the mother would have no more children.

Cholera came in cycles — about every seven years. As soon as a dead rat fell from the roof of a hut, the people fled, spreading the dreaded bubonic plague to the next village. They regarded these epidemics as the appearance of an evil god. To placate this god, the first victim was left to die. All night long and into the early morning there was the noise of beating tom-toms and shouting to a god to rid them of the disease. The people thought their loud wailing kept the evil spirits away; they would shout epithets and beat the idols who refused to help. But they would not kill the rats because they believed them to be the embodiment of the spirits of those who had died in previous famines. Because they did not get enough to eat during their lives on earth, they had returned to make up for lost time.

Bethesda Hospital was founded primarily to combat the appalling number of childbirth and infant deaths. Women were considered worthless and ignorant and would not let male doctors treat them. Often patients were brought to the hospital as a last resort, after all the superstitious rites had failed or the village midwives, with their sometimes brutal methods and utter lack of cleanliness, had done their worst. It was heartbreaking when all that could be done was to make a dying woman comfortable. "My saddest experience in India," Angela said, "is to care for the woman with a ruptured uterus who has traveled by oxcart over rutted roads, from far distances, for hospital care. When she arrives with no pulse, we work fast to revive her. When she leaves the hospital to return to her village, we see the miracle of God's help in our medical mission work.

"At Bethesda," she added, "we must keep the mothers seven to nine days after childbirth, for they do not have proper care in their homes, where the earth is the floor and there are no lavatory facilities. Many of the poor, undernourished mothers have little or no breast milk for their infants. If there is milk to be purchased, the parents are too poor to buy it. Often in the second or third month of breast-feeding the baby gets thinner and thinner and finally dies of starvation."

Diseases included malaria, diphtheria, dysentery, arthritis, rheumatism, anemia, nephritis, snake and scorpion bites, tuberculosis, leprosy, hookworms and roundworms, broken bones, toothaches, sprains, scabies, gastritis, cataracts. During cholera or plague epidemics, the hospital staff worked overtime giving inoculations; and some of the missionaries also volunteered their services. Much suffering was caused by tiny gnats that were attracted to open sores, particularly to the eyes. Hookworms would enter bodies. Little children came with boils all over their heads; it was very painful for them to have their heads shaved and cleaned. A woman with boils on both cheeks came to the hospital. Her mother-in-law and two sisters-in-law shaved their heads and sacrificed the hair to an idol. They credited that, rather than the medical treatment, for her recovery.

When a patient came to Bethesda Hospital, his relatives accompanied him, and some would stay to prepare the meals and care for him. They brought food supplies and their mats and slept under the beds. (The hospital drew the line at live chickens tied to the bedpost.) In her own kitchen, Angela prepared food for those needing special diets. Hospital beds were frightening to the patients who thought they were being placed on dangerously high shelves; they would sometimes wrap sheets around themselves and take refuge on the floor. One morning a man came to the hospital and asked that someone come right away to see the wife of his friend. Angela found a pregnant woman, in a large, well-kept house, lying on the floor, hemorrhaging, with a pulse of 103. Angela told the family the woman would not live unless they brought her to the hospital. There she was given an intravenous injection and made comfortable. Later that evening the nurse-midwife delivered her baby, after which the mother's pulse was very low, and Angela did not think she could possibly survive. Throughout the long night Angela frequently checked her. By morning the young mother had begun to improve. During the two weeks of recovery, the mother-in-law, always dressed in the finest of saris, stayed at the hospital. Angela told her many times that it was only through the help of God that her daughter-in-law had been saved. All the woman would say was, "I have faith in you." How much the Word took root no one knew.

Missionary wife Kathy Michalk remembers an outbreak of bubonic plague. A child of the mission's Training School headmaster found a dead rat and brought it home to show her mother; the girl and a sibling died soon after, and their mother was brought to Bethesda Hospital. Until immunizations were developed, bubonic plague meant almost certain death as muscular paralysis attacked the entire system. Angela refused to give up. She and the Indian nurses fed, cared for and prayed for the woman; her heart and lungs kept functioning, and after a period of many months, the woman was able to go home to her family. That same careful, prayerful nursing enabled Angela to boast that she had never lost a typhoid patient.

In a nearby village a Christian man was married to a Hindu woman, whose influence had kept their children from being baptized. When she was about to deliver her twelfth child, the wife's condition became critical and the local midwives gave up the case in despair. "I happened to be in the neighborhood that night," reported Missionary H. Manns, "and I brought her to the Ambur hospital. The next morning she was delivered of her child and, humanly speaking, rescued from death. I have been informed that the child will be brought to baptism."

Another time a very sick man was brought to the hospital. He was not expected to live. The missionary came to see him often and baptized him. The man did recover and went home a changed man (he had been a drunkard). He felt sorry that he could not give something to show his appreciation but said he would come back some day. Nearly three years passed. One Sunday evening the man and his wife and children appeared. They put a large garland around Angela's neck and presented her with a plate of fruit and sweets. The man gave a little speech, thanking her for her care three years earlier, and sprinkled her with rosewater.

Hospital patients were billed for their care, but most of them were very poor. If they could not pay the five to twenty cents for one day's medicine, they were treated free. A few of the upper caste people with good incomes deliberately donned old, torn clothing, removed their jewelry and posed as poor villagers who needed "Christian charity." Angela developed an uncanny ability to recognize the disguises, and so gently and tactfully did she get them to pay the modest fees that they usually took it in good grace.

Sometimes a dependable village woman would be shown how to administer pills or eye drops. Only a few days' medication would be given to outpatients, some of whom reasoned that if one pill a day healed over a period of time, taking the whole bottle at once would bring an instant cure!

Work to Angela was more important than talk. "Dramatic experiences do not happen very often," she said, agreeing with missionary Amy Carmichael that "there isn't much of a halo in real life." But Angela didn't care about halos. Angela worked; Angela stayed.

IV. Orphans

Angela loved children. The oldest girl in a widowed pastor's family, she mothered her six siblings even after her father remarried. Her American nieces and nephews, many of whom met her for the first time when she came back from India on furlough, received gifts specially selected for each of them. A niece remembers Angela gathering the children around the organ for hymn sings. "From Greenland's Icy Mountains" was

Angela's favorite, and the children knew that when she sang the second line, "to India's coral strand," or when she chided them to clean their plates because the starving children in India could feast on their garbage, their aunt was speaking from first-hand experience.

Angela could not bear to see a child suffer. In addition to the patients, Bethesda Hospital usually housed one or more small orphans who would have perished without Angela's tender "adoption." Angela began saving for an orphanage at Bethesda (which never materialized) and although she was usually reticent and shy about talking about her work, she spoke to many women's groups during her furloughs in the United States. "Forty dollars will support a child for one year at the mission boarding schools where the older orphans are sent," she boldly challenged them.

In March 1930 Angela wrote, "There is only one orphan now that has not a stipend, and that is a little four-year old boy who is staying here at the hospital. He was baptized by Rev. Stevenson and given the name John Sundrum — but everybody calls him Thambi. He is a fine looking fellow, healthy and strong and very affectionate, and I just love him!

"So far the mission has taken care of 20 children, but many are not full orphans; they either have a mother or a father," continued Angela. "When I came back from furlough last year, Louise Rathke [a deaconess who came to Bethesda in late 1926 to relieve Angela for her furlough] had taken in a widow and her three daughters who all were sick because they had not enough to eat. They seem improved and the mother wanted to stay here. She had been under

The little orphan Thambi

instruction in her village and wished to become a Christian. So we kept her, gave her some work, and she and the children are now ready to be baptized. The oldest girl is about six years old and has learned some prayers and songs. The second girl is about three. I wish you could hear her pray the prayer, 'Ich bin eine kleine Kinderlein' ('I am a little child' — in Tamil rather than German or English, of course). The youngest one says, 'Abba, amen.' She is nearly two and cannot walk. The woman seems very good at her work and has been anxious to study, but we never know how long this lasts. So often the mothers become dissatisfied and go back to their villages."

One day Louise went to the railroad station to pick up medicine. "Can you take these children?" asked the agent, pointing to two huddled waifs — a girl about eight with a rag around her hips and a naked smaller boy. Someone had put them off a train going through Ambur. Louise took them to the hospital, bathed, fed and clothed them and waited for relatives. None came.

A Muslim woman gave birth to a baby at Bethesda Hospital. The following day she offered it to Angela. The father of the child had left her several months previous, she was too poor to take care of it properly, and she was determined to give her daughter to Christians, not Muslims, because, she said, "I know you will be kind to my baby." A Christian family from a village about 25 miles from Ambur adopted the child, and the mother left the hospital in a happy frame of mind.

In 1934 a coworker wrote, "The latest news is that a *pariah* (outcast) dog has adopted Miss Rehwinkel. Not only the dogs are fond of her, but the babies flock to her also." (She was commenting on the birth of triplets at the hospital.) A succession of labrador retrievers replaced the stray. When Kathy and Ted Michalk arrived in India in 1945, Angela was on furlough, and they were temporarily assigned to her rooms in the mission's women's bungalow. Angela's dog Rusty was being

Angela and her dog

cared for by Louise Rathke, who occupied the other half of the house. But Rusty missed his mistress, and anytime the door was left ajar he would sneak in and sprawl out on Angela's bed, which he vacated only reluctantly. Kathy didn't appreciate repeatedly shaking the bedspread to get rid of dog hair. Rusty was Angela's guardian and devoted slave. The other missionaries dubbed him "Mr. Rehwinkel," an affectionate jibe at the courtliness with which Angela always addressed her coworkers. Every afternoon at exactly 4:00 Angela would sit in her office and watch as the huge dog sedately strolled down the road from her bungalow, a basket containing her tea and snack carefully held in his mouth.

Orphans were not the only recipients of Angela's and Louise's kindness. A number of older widows, who received charity from the mission, were being victimized by relatives who took the women's meager food allowances. Two empty storage rooms were cleared and a miniature "old ladies' home" was established on the hospital compound; food was prepared by the woman who cooked for the orphans.

"Our Old Ladies' Home was not in existence very long," wrote Louise. "One of the women became ill the first night here and, as she was very superstitious, she claimed the devil had come in the shape of a horse and kicked her, which accounted for her illness. Besides that problem, relatives and friends could not come to visit the women every day, and the women seemed to miss them so much. Nearly every day they gave a different reason for wanting to go back to their villages. They said they had come only to get the sari promised by the missionaries if they came to live here. We did all we could to make things pleasant for them, but one Sunday morning, when they noticed that nobody was paying special attention to them, they took 'French leave,' without even saying *salaam*."

All of the orphans Angela "adopted" became members of the India Lutheran Church and kept in touch with her. Thambi invited her to his wedding.

V. The Bible Women

Angela never lost sight of the primary purpose of medical missions: to bring the message of Jesus' love to the people of India. Every morning, when most of the outpatients had gathered on the veranda, there was a brief devotion. Angela played the organ, the hospital staff sang a hymn and Samuel, the compounder (pharmacist), read a Tamil portion of Scripture. The waiting people either listened or walked away. Later Bible women distributed Bible pictures and verses and talked to the waiting women. Each patient received a Gospel *chit* — a receipt with a short message of salvation through Jesus Christ printed on the back.

Bible women played a key role in bringing the Gospel to India. Muslim and high-caste Hindu men did not allow other men to teach or visit their women. As early as 1871 Christian missions were training women who could read and write (many of them widows or wives of teachers in the mission boarding schools) in basic theology and teaching skills. It was these Bible women who brought the Word to many women and children of India.

After Dr. Doederlein left India, Angela's coworker Lula Ellermann devoted her time to visiting women in their homes, demonstrating basic cleanliness and hygiene. She also trained Bible women. In 1924 Lula wrote about her first recruit, a widow named Ratinamal: "About 17 years ago a man and woman with two children came through the village where Ratinamal and her husband lived. They happened to stop in front of Ratinamal's house and said their baby was possessed by a devil. He was six months old. Since his birth they had had nothing but trouble, and now their house had burned down. They said they must get rid of him. Even though they loved their son, their god was not pleased with him. Ratinamal and her husband were delighted to have a baby. So this is Moses, now 17 or 18 years old. He is not a boy who learns easily from books, but it seemed he wanted to learn some trade, so I made inquiries and found a good motor mechanic school in Madras and paid six-months' tuition as my contribution to the mission."

Ratinamal and Lula travelled together, sharing the good news of Jesus. Lula did not return to India after her second furlough in 1926. Instead she married Joe Sundermann and settled down in Clarinda, Iowa.

A Bible woman at work

Deaconess Louise Rathke took over the Bible women work, laboring faithfully for more than 35 years. She solicited new recruits and conducted training sessions. She also taught the women to read and to sew. By 1928 the Ambur mission had 11 Bible women who made a total of 1,739 calls during the year. Louise described their work: "One day I started out with two Bible women to visit one of the villages. I sent one of them to instruct the catechumens. There is not one woman who can read or write. Everything has to be learned by rote. The other Bible woman and I went from house to house, calling the women together. The women sat on the sand-covered floor of the schoolhouse, and we began our weekly lesson with a Bible story. At times lively discussion arose, sometimes offering deep insights into their lives. The story of Jesus feeding the 5,000 appealed to them particularly, and one of them said, 'If we were in the desert or jungle, the idol gods would not help us; they would let us starve to death.' Another time a woman hearing the ages of the Bible patriarchs exclaimed, 'What a long time to suffer!'

"Munisi was an old woman; her hair had turned gray many years ago. The Bible women had visited her for many years. She often said she wanted to be a Christian some day, but not yet. One day the Bible woman replied, 'You have told us that now for seven years. You are getting old. Someday you must die. Then what? Don't you think you'd better do something about it soon?' The words struck home. Munisi began to study and was baptized. That was a great day for her. Even though she has to make her own living by cleaning rice, frying little cakes for sale or doing any kind of odd jobs around the houses, she is always happy to see us and has time to sit and listen.

"An illiterate woman asked one day, 'Have you any more of these little books?' (tracts). 'Why, yes,' said the Bible woman. 'Why do you want one?' She replied, 'Since my husband has read them, wisdom has come to him. He does not beat me anymore. Won't you give me some more books so that more wisdom will come to him?' Said another, 'We Hindu women are afraid of our husbands. We have to serve them with fear. With you Christians it is different. You love!'"

On Easter Day in 1937 Ratinamal, the first Bible woman, had a cerebral hemorrhage. Louise told the story: "For many weeks her whole left side was paralyzed, but now she is walking around a little, though she is still very weak. She is living with her adopted son, Moses, who is our mechanic and my driver. I think she is well taken care of, as her daughter-in-law Gnanapu (who was also training to be a Bible woman) waits on her. It is very difficult for Ratinamal now — she has been active all her life — to spend most of her time lying or sitting. She was a faithful servant in the Lord's kingdom for over 20 years."

One morning Louise noticed a servant talking to herself while hoeing the garden. "Rangamma," Louise asked, "what are you saying?" "Amma," was the reply, "I am studying to become a Christian." Louise was surprised. For many years the seed of God's Word had not seemed to bear fruit in this woman. "Has Christ come to your house?" Louise asked. "And do you want to study to be baptized?" When Rangamma answered affirmatively, Louise said, "Then you can go to Ratinamal, the Bible woman. She can instruct you during the noon hour." Rangamma faithfully went almost daily to Ratinamal's house and studied for her baptism day. In spite of paralysis, Ratinamal was still able to serve her Lord.

Angela, too, felt that talking directly to people about the Savior was of first importance. In 1924 Angela taught a women's sewing class at the hospital. While the women learned their stitches, a Bible woman talked to them. When she could spare the time, Angela went with the Bible women as they visited villages. A car was provided the women missionaries at Ambur in 1930, and Louise energetically buzzed around the countryside, delighted at the opportunity to reach more women in farther villages. But Angela stayed with familiar ways and traveled in "Black Moriah."

VI. Nurses and Doctors

Nurses Angela and Lula, together with Anna Georgi who arrived at Ambur in 1921 to supervise the girls' boarding school, lived in one of the mission-owned bungalows with Missionary Frederick Blaess's family. Lula and Angela alternated sleeping at the hospital, and they all shared the bungalow's kitchen. Such crowding sometimes caused personality clashes. Wrote Lula: "Miss Georgi, Miss Rehwinkel and I are together as a family would be at home at meal time and a little while in the evening. I get along with all of the ladies, but ...!" (Missionary Blaess complained that these crowded living arrangements were making his wife very nervous.) "As to Miss Rehwinkel," Lula hastened to add, "there is not a finer girl than she. She is good company and very conscientious in her work."

After returning to the United States, Dr. Doederlein gathered $6,000, and in 1926 a separate bungalow for the unmarried women workers was added to the Ambur compound. But Angela continued to sleep at the hospital because she did not want her young Indian nurse to be left alone at night. Anna Georgi had a bout with dengue fever, and she did not tolerate the tropical heat. After five years she went home on furlough and did not return to India. She was replaced by a succession of nurses, teachers and deaconesses.

Through the more than 37 years of Angela's service, a total of 11 single women came to Ambur. Some could not adjust to the climate or the Indian culture and soon left; others stayed longer.

A few met and married male missionaries. Angela welcomed all of them. Modest about her own accomplishments, she suggested, "I really would be glad if a younger nurse just recently out of training would take charge of the hospital. There is so much to do, and I can go out to a village and work where a younger nurse would feel terribly misused." But the short stay of many of them prompted her to write: "Any young lady coming to the mission field should have some training in mission work and

Angela and two Indian nurses with triplets born at Bethesda Hospital

should not be sent out here just for the glamour of it. There must be some consecration in this work."

Angela's humility and consideration extended to her Indian coworkers. Bethesda Hospital tended many pregnant women and had a good reputation for safe childbirths. Boasted Angela, "My Indian nurses have spent several months studying midwifery after they had their nurses' training, and they are very capable." When the Mission Board found it necessary to cut salaries, Angela begged them not include the Indian hospital employees who so badly needed the money. Once while on furlough she sent a special request to the American Mission Board: "The compounder at our hospital will be with us 25 years next February 1947. I feel that a greeting from the Board to show his work has been appreciated would mean much to him. He has been honest and loyal in his work."

Dr. Davadasan, the native doctor, was a Christian gentleman; his wife was a member of the Lutheran Church and he later also joined. But the medical education he had received in India was not as advanced as that of his American counterparts. He was trained to do only minor surgery; serious cases were referred to the Christian Medical College Hospital at Vellore, 30 miles away. Angela often found herself knowing treatments and procedures better than he. In the Indian caste system, lighter color gives status. Angela was tall, fair and strawberry blonde; Dr. Davadasan was shorter and dark-skinned. It took a great deal of tact to make constructive suggestions without appearing condescending.

From the time Dr. Doederlein left, Angela pleaded for another American doctor, preferably a woman. In 1932, eight years later, Dr. Eleanor Bohnsack was commissioned by the Mission Board to serve at the Ambur Hospital. Angela was delighted. For her orientation to tropical medicine, Dr. Bohnsack went to Calcutta where leprosy was being researched. She was enthusiastic about starting a sanitarium at Bethesda Hospital. Angela readily admitted that Ambur was full of leprosy: "I know a village about two miles from Ambur where you will find a leper in nearly every home. Not many days pass that we do not see a leper standing in front of our hospital anxiously waiting his turn for treatment. Dr. Davadasan and I both are able to recognize a leper as soon as we see one." But Angela advised caution. As long as they were able to work, lepers were allowed to live with their families. Most of them refused isolation; some went to existing sanitariums during the rainy season but preferred to beg the rest of the time. Because the treatment was painful and drawn-out, others would not return to the hospital for the free weekly injections of chaulmoogra oil. After two years of service, Eleanor Bohnsack married Dr. Glenn Crimm, an American dentist practicing in Madras, and she left Ambur.

Angela had her times of discouragement. "The day has only 12 hours and the week only seven days, and my body is often so tired that even that seems long. Our hospital work is of the nature that you either have to get away from it or work all the time," she wrote. "It often seems as if we are out here for nothing and are just using up money that our friends in America send. But," she added, "the Lord is gracious to us and knows what we need."

The hospital had its ups and downs. Workers came and went. Angela stayed.

VII. The Journeys of Absalom

Dr. Doederlein had recruited a 1924 seminary graduate, Norbert Leckband, to study medicine and go to India. Before his training in Chicago was completed, the future doctor became engaged to Meta Schrader, a deaconess trainee for India. Meta felt she could honor her commitment for one term; she came to Ambur in 1927 with two deaconess classmates, Elsie Mahler and Clara Mueller, who soon met and married single male missionaries. Being a bridesmaid while her sweetheart was an ocean away was too much for Meta; her fellow-missionaries loaned her $500 so she could return to the United States. In 1929 she and Norbert married, and soon there was a baby on the way. Entering medicine with a child, a wife who had bouts of malaria and a debt in India concerned the young doctor. He begged for a few years to become solvent before taking on a missionary's salary. When he felt financially able, the Mission Board was strapped for money. Finally in 1936 Dr. Norbert Leckband and his family arrived at Bethesda Hospital, only a few months after the death of the Dr. Davadasan. Angela mourned the death of her friend but was delighted to welcome the new doctor.

Shortly after beginning his duties, Dr. Leckband wrote, "Our fine little hospital-dispensary occupies a warm spot in the hearts of everyone in Ambur — Hindu, Mohammedan and Christian alike. This position of respect in the community is due largely to the conscientious devotion and hard work of Miss Rehwinkel, of whose activities as superintendent not enough superlatives could be written."

An ambulance was purchased with monies donated by women in Fort Wayne, Indiana. Missionary Manns christened it Absalom "because he gets his hair [roof-top] in the tree branches all the time." Absalom quickly became the "talk of the town in Vellakottai, Nimmiyampet, Korndampet,

"Absalom"—the ambulance and mobile dispensary

Gunalapalti, Yerukkampattu, Battlepali, Venkatasamundram — even though such unheard-of villages as New York and Chicago don't know about him. He goes out into the highways and hedges with his pills and powders and sometimes compels the lame and halt to come to the hospital." Dr. Leckband loved this dispensary work, and Angela was pleased that the accompanying Bible women and sometimes missionaries were spreading the Gospel in the villages. The task of staying behind to manage the hospital fell to Angela. So, of course, she stayed.

In late 1941 the Japanese bombed Rangoon, Burma. There were more than 3,000 casualties as Japanese bombers descended and machine-gunned people in the streets. Corpses floated down the river to be left under the wharves for days. One Methodist missionary in Rangoon picked up 25 bodies from in front of his house. Burmese doctors and nurses deserted their posts, leaving hospital patients with no care. The governor of Madras, India, asked Doctor Galen Scudder to head a medical team going to Burma, and he in turn asked his friend Norbert Leckband to accompany him. They arrived in Rangoon early the next year in the midst of an air raid, but the Flying Tigers had preceded them and the worst of the carnage was over. This experience had a profound impact on Dr. Leckband. When rumors circulated that India was to be Japan's next target, he brought his family back to the United States. Once again Angela stayed to work — with two doctors, two male and five female nurses, a lab technician, cleaning staff and a night watchman, all Indian.

Angela's boundless energy had limits. In 1942 a thorn prick became infected, and it took six long, painful surgeries to save her left thumb. Afterwards she was very tired but felt the hospital could not spare her for a furlough. Her friends insisted she needed a rest — they would carry on; the hospital would survive this difficult time as it had in the past. So in 1945 Angela booked passage on a ship to America. World War II was barely over, and there was danger on the high seas;

all women passengers were ordered to wear slacks en route. Angela was dismayed! She had always worn skirts! Besides, wasn't there something in the Bible forbidding women to wear men's clothes? It took some persuasion by missionary Martin Kretzmann that Deuteronomy 22:5 need not be translated so literally. "I must say," he said, "Angela looked very handsome and trim in those slacks." Though it was difficult to continue the dispensaries, the hospital staff and missionary volunteers managed to keep Absalom on the road.

VIII. A Dream Realized

In 1950 Dr. Wolfgang and Gisella Bulle, survivors of Nazi rule in Germany, arrived in Ambur. A most welcome supply of surgical, obstetric and x-ray equipment was sent with them. A year later the Lutheran Women's Missionary League (LWML) convention pledged $70,000 to expand Bethesda. At the same convention Angela was cited for 30 years of service at the hospital. She felt honored by the recognition but was too busy to travel to New York to receive the award. She was much more excited about the anticipated enlarged hospital.

Young Dr. Bulle entered his new responsibilities with vigor and enthusiasm. "The medical mission work at Ambur is not

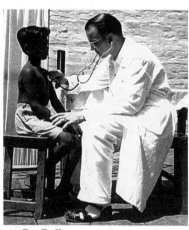

Dr. Bulle examining a patient

only the life task I have chosen and out of which I'd like to make as much as I possibly can, but much more, it is the Lord's work for which only the highest standards should be good enough," he wrote. "Luke 9:2, 'And He sent them to preach the kingdom of God and to heal the sick,' is what Bethesda Hospital has been doing — 4,900 patients treated last year by two Indian doctors and some nurses!" Dr. Bulle reported that the obstetrical department was well run. "After seeing circumstances out here with my own eyes, I still more admire the courage and continuous endeavors of Miss Rehwinkel, without whom the present hospital would not exist."

In addition to a grueling surgery schedule, Dr. Bulle superintended all of the details of remodeling and building a new, modern hospital. It was not unusual for him to begin the day at 7:00 a.m. with a full eight hours of surgery and then work until 2:00 a.m. with carpenters and suppliers and blueprints. There was a typhoid outbreak and a famine in 1952, and Dr. Bulle supervised the distribution of relief packages. "Right now we have seven children with almost the worst possible form of typhoid," he reported. "I can say at least three would have died if we had not supplemented their diet with milk. About 90 children, which I picked out as being especially in need, are getting milk every evening at my bungalow. It is a real joy to see how different some of these kids look after they have been on milk for about two months."

Included in the new hospital were a new outpatient department, an operating theater and x-ray plant; an extension of the Indian nurses' homes; a second floor on the surgery building; residences for doctors and compounders; kitchens for patients and their relatives; an electric substation, incinerator and water system; and a laundry with adjoining drying yard. "The hot water for the laundry comes now from an electric boiling room and need not any longer be heated on half-open, smoky clay stoves fed with expensive wood," rejoiced Angela.

Dedication day was January 25, 1955. The governor of Madras, Sri Sra Pragasa, was present to make a speech and cut the ribbon. Dr. Ida B. Scudder, founder of the Vellore Christian Medical College, was an honored guest. The new outpatient building was dedicated to the memory of Dr. Theodore Doederlein; the unveiling of a memorial plaque in honor of Angela was included in the ceremony.

Bethesda Hospital in the early 1950s

For such a special occasion, Angela eschewed her starched white uniform and wore a beautiful new sari. Gisella Bulle described the gala: "The festivities included a charity sale, carnival, exhibitions, tours of the hospital, two dinners at the nurses bungalow for 100 plus, and a formal dinner for the governor at our house. All the older buildings were freshly whitewashed, and a 15-foot long *pandel* (open tent with bamboo posts and a palm leaf roof) was erected. The roof was covered underneath with white cloth and edged with hundreds of yards of blue and red fringes with gold borders. The bamboo poles were wound with flowers and colored paper laces. Carpets led to the stage, and 1,000 chairs left a long aisle where the governor walked to open the gate of the hospital."

Gisella and her helpers had painted the bathroom, scrubbed the bungalow and polished the floor in anticipation of their distinguished guest. Her children were excited about the "king" who was coming to their house and expected a gold crown and a wonder of a car (they weren't disappointed by the latter). "In spite of the fanfare," said Gisella, "I saw him as another nice houseguest, lonely and rather old."

Next day the governor presided at the cornerstone laying of a branch hospital at Reddivlasu, a rural area 25 miles from

Ambur. This new facility was funded by the Indian government's "rural uplift" program; a local man donated the land. As soon as the Reddivalasu Branch Hospital was completed, Nurse Hedwig Gronbach, recently arrived in India, was placed in charge.

Angela's hard work at Bethesda and perseverance had finally paid off! Her dream had come true, and she was excited. She knew her retirement was not too many years away, and she wrote, "There does not seem to be any letup in the work that Dr. Bulle is planning. I get very tired, although I still look after a great deal of the work outside nursing. Perhaps I should give up this work now so that the younger people can take hold and do it the way of the present times."

But she didn't really mean it, and she was reassured by the Mission Board: "You are so necessary to our hospital that no one we know will be able to replace you." Dr. Bulle added, "We need Miss Rehwinkel more than ever before; perhaps not to do so much of the practical work but to advise our younger, less experienced people. I can operate on a patient but cannot at the same time pray or talk to the family frozen in terror or anguish. It will not be easy to find a successor for Miss Rehwinkel," he added. "The person required would definitely have to be of rather superior qualities."

Once the hospital was built, Dr. Bulle turned his energies to a five-year plan for further improvements. "We do not know how much time we have left," he wrote. "Bethesda Hospital will survive the political changes in this country only if it is self-supporting, modernly equipped and run by a well-trained Indian staff." With funds from Wheat Ridge Ministries, a mobile x-ray unit was purchased. The Indian government funded a mass tuberculosis survey and inoculation program for the entire city of Ambur. A mobile clinic was donated by the Iowa East LWML.

Another of Angela's dreams was realized when in 1953 missionary Robert Trautmann came from Krishnigiri to be full-time chaplain at Bethesda Hospital. His first task was to train Indian Pastor J. Isaiah as his successor.

For more than 30 years, Angela had been chief financial officer, purchasing agent and nursing supervisor. She had managed very well as long as there were only 30 or so beds. But suddenly 120 beds and burgeoning surgery, plus tuberculosis and leprosy care, were overwhelming. Angela was always very careful with money and the accounting of it, but her bookkeeping and filing methods were hardly modern. Missionary Grumm remembers that when he drove Angela to Vellore to save her infected thumb, she anxiously told him where she had hidden various monies saved for special purchases. Missionary Trautmann helped organize the hospital's financial records and gradually took on more of the administration. His last task before leaving Bethesda in 1959 was to train Mr. G. Samuel as the hospital's first non-medical administrator.

For Angela the years were beginning to take their toll. In 1955 her "zoological garden" of accumulated tropical germs brought her typhoid fever. She found it difficult and discouraging to take time for her own slow healing. While recuperating she fell over an open desk drawer and broke her hip. Spending almost six months in a wheel chair and on crutches, Angela realized her tired body was wearing out. In 1956 she wrote the Mission Board: "The time has come for me to resign."

Angela had stayed and stayed. Now Angela went home. On January 12, 1959, at the age of 76, she returned to the United States. At her retirement gala in Ambur, she was presented with many gifts, as well as a printed copy of the speech given by a member of the hospital staff: "We, the members of the staff of Bethesda Hospital, look to your departure from us with feelings of thankfulness and praise, yet also with great sadness. As we look back on many days and years of close friendship and association with you, we recognize ... the many thousands who have received your careful and loving care ... the many mothers and babies who received your untiring attention; the thousands who have come here afflicted with deathly typhoid, cholera and smallpox, and walked away well; the orphaned babies who still today remember only you as their mother. All these join us in praise and thanks to our gracious God who brought you to us and has kept you with us for so many years."

Angela is honored upon her retirement from Bethesda Hospital

IX. Endings

Angela's nursing did not end with her retirement. Returning to the United States, she found that her sister-in-law, Dr. Bessie Rehwinkel, had suffered a stroke and her brother Alfred was "cook, housemaid, day and night nurse, and very tired." Angela joined the St. Louis household, and the burden was lessened considerably. After Bessie's death two years later, Angela stayed to keep house for her brother. As she became older and more feeble, their roles reversed, and Alfred became the "nurse." In 1972 Angela was moved to a nursing home in Kendallville, Indiana. On September 22 she celebrated her 90th birthday at her brother Rudolph's Kendallville home. She died on May 27, 1973. When the news reached Ambur, the non-emergency hospital staff took a holiday to mourn her death.

Bethesda Hospital continues as a haven for the sick in the Ambur area. The property is owned by the India Evangelical Lutheran Church Trust Association and is well run by Indian staff. It continues to serve many patients, and in 1994 it showed the largest income in its history. Sadly, since it is no longer supported by mission donations, the hospital has had to limit charity patients.

"When Missionary Naether went to Krishnigari in 1895, it was six years before he baptized his first convert," says Nurse Alice Brauer, the only LCMS missionary still serving in India. "The church there has grown very slowly. Within a three-mile radius of Ambur, on the other hand, there are seven Lutheran churches and a very strong Christian presence. I would like to attribute some of that to the ministry of Bethesda Hospital. In India, Christ is often known as the healing God."

Epilogue

As chance would have it, Sigmund Hillmer was a pastor in Corunna, Indiana, and his wife Ellen was a nurse at the nearby Kendallville hospital where, near the end of her life, Angela was admitted as a patient. "When I walked into her room and told her who I was," says Ellen, "she opened her arms for a big hug as she exclaimed, 'My baby!'" And it was Pastor Hillmer and Angela's nephew, Pastor Eugene Rehwinkel, who officiated at Angela's funeral at St. John's Lutheran Church, Kendallville, Indiana, on May 30, 1973. "What a great lady she was!" exclaims Ellen. "I thank the Lord for Angela Rehwinkel!"

Louise Mueller has written devotions for Portals of Prayer, *Bible studies for the LWML and is former editor-in-chief of the* Lutheran Woman's Quarterly. *She has three adult children and lives in St. Louis, Missouri, with her husband Howard.*

In India Where Roses Bloom

by Rose Ziemke

"Bed tea, Madam?" I opened my eyes. A little dark man in a clean white suit and neatly wrapped turban was rolling up my mosquito net. I was in India — my very first morning. It was December 28, 1947.

I had traveled with Hans and Marie Naumann, their four children and Herb and Dorothy Zorn from San Francisco to Madras on a converted troop ship called the Marine Swallow (we called it the Marine Wallow). The only converting they did was to remove the guns. We were on that ship over a month — 350 missionaries, a few businessmen and a few people headed for consulates in Burma, Thailand or India.

Now I suddenly found myself completely alone, far from home, in a strange land — and a strange man was in my room! The hotel where we stayed that night was filled and I, the only single person in our party, was given a room on the ground floor in back of the kitchen. I was surprised and a little fearful. But I was being treated to an old British custom — bed tea!

The trip to India was rough. We sailed under the Golden Gate Bridge the day after Thanksgiving. The Pacific Ocean in the wintertime is anything but peaceful. We had to go out of our way to avoid a thousand-mile storm front, but the weather was still blustery and cold. Twenty-six women and children slept on bunk beds in one cabin. The men were in cabins away in the bow of the ship — a sad arrangement for newlyweds Herb and Dorothy Zorn. I was fortunate to get a bunk by the wall, and since there was no one in the upper bunk I hung up a blanket behind which I could dress and undress with a degree of privacy.

I was also fortunate that I did not suffer, as many did, from seasickness. My sister, an army nurse, had been issued warm clothing for the European theater and was then sent to the Philippines. She gave me all the warm clothes I needed to spend my days out on deck — unless it got very bad and we were ordered to our cabins.

We went ashore in Shanghai, Hong Kong and Singapore. In Shanghai we dined in a restaurant with Missionary R. J. Mueller and family and two couples who had been in mission school with Herb, Dorothy and me. The meal for nine of us was a cool million dollars, Shanghai dollars that is! In Hong Kong we went shopping and took a taxi to the top of a hill overlooking the harbor. What a beautiful view! On the ship I had met and enjoyed the company of Helen and George Schaeffer, missionaries with the American Lutheran Mission, who were returning to India. In Singapore they took me to a lovely dinner at the home of Dr. Oh, who had an eye clinic next door.

It had been so grim on the ship, the missionaries decided we should do all we could to celebrate Christmas. With the help of the crew we did some decorating, and a Christmas Eve service was conducted. I discovered that the two young priests Eunice Naumann and I had played cards with were setting up for Christmas Eve Midnight Mass.

"Would you like to use the white cloth I bought in Hong Kong on your altar?" I asked. "Yes!" was the reply.

So my white-on-white embroidered grass linen tablecloth was used on the make-shift altar for Midnight Mass. One of the young priests had a beautiful tenor voice. We stood at the door, listening with rapture as he sang "Jesu, Bambino."

Later I stood at the rail as the ship slipped silently through the Bay of Bengal. Looking up at the beautiful star-filled sky, I was moved almost to tears. Now I understood the true meaning of "Silent Night, Holy Night."

Two days later we landed in Madras, India.

From Madras to Trivandrum

Herb and Dorothy Zorn and I traveled by train to Trivandrum, Kerala (in those days called Travancore). It was mostly desert until we crossed the Madras state border. Then it was coconut palms everywhere, and the agriculture was mainly tapioca and yams.

We were welcomed in Trivandrum by all the local missionaries at a get-together supper. At a meeting afterward I was asked to teach at the school for missionary children on Loch End Compound, Kodaikanal. The teacher who was called was not coming, and since I had not started my work I was the logical one to take over the school — grades one to eight. The seventh and eighth graders were taking some classes at a nearby junior high, so I would have them only part of the day. I had taught kindergarten and first and second grades; now I was being asked to teach upper grades. Naturally I was worried, but then I remembered the Lord does not ask more of us than, with His help, we are able to do.

Two weeks later I again found myself on the train, this time for Kodaikanal in the Palani Hills. Overnight on an Indian train is something else! I made the mistake of getting into pajamas and going to bed. At 6:00 a.m. the doors opened and people poured in to sit with us.

At Kodaikanal Road station we left the train and boarded a bus for the 7,500-foot climb up the mountain. We ascended 3,000 feet the first ten miles. Twenty more miles of hairpin curves one after the other, and then we felt the cool air and smelled the eucalyptus wood burning.

Up on the Mountain

I enjoyed teaching at Kodaikanal immensely. I took my meals with the children but had rooms in one of the small cottages — rooms I almost immediately began decorating with one or two carved tables, a small Bokara rug and other Indian artifacts. The children spent ten months of the year in school. Hill leave for the missionaries was during the hot season (usually April and May). Then they came to Kodaikanal where cottages on two compounds were available. Parents could take their children out of boarding to be with them for six weeks. Later the children would have two months with their parents during the cool season.

My year in Kodaikanal went fast. I hated to leave so much beauty — the flowers, the walk around the lake, the church services, the friends. At the same time I was anxiously looking forward to starting the work for which I had come to India.

Rose Ziemke during her early years in India

During the year I spent teaching in Kodaikanal, earth-shaking events took place: independence ... an end to British rule ... an end to the old regime ... the maharajahs would take a back seat to democratic rule. Mahatma Gandhi was shot. There was trouble all over India as the new government tried to unite a new nation. There were tremendous problems trying to appease both the Hindus and the Muslims. There would be many new laws, many changes.

In years to come, whenever I went to Kodaikanal for hill leave, I tried to get there for Easter. I have beautiful memories of Easter in Kodaikanal. The singers going past at 4:00 a.m. declaring, "Christ is risen, hallelujah!" At 5:00 a.m. singing Easter hymns and watching the sunrise high above the plains. From all the different missions — the Swedish, the German, the London Mission, the United Lutheran, the American Lutheran — missionaries gathered to celebrate. A truly mountain-top experience! Then the Missouri Evangelical Lutheran India Mission (MELIM) missionaries had breakfast in the rock garden, and after breakfast we had a worship service in our own beautiful stone church. Easter lilies grew profusely and the altar was filled with them. Often a large cross of lilies was made by the children.

Down on the Plains

One of the first things I discovered before starting my work among Indian women was that I needed help. It was difficult to find a good *munshi*, language teacher. Although English was still in use in government and public places and by educated people, the women with whom I would be working knew very little or no English. In fact most were illiterate. I needed to learn Malayalam, the language of the Kerala area, and I needed to learn it fast.

A high school teacher, Davidas, was hired to be my *munshi*. Since Davidas had no experience teaching language and no material with which to work, I suggested we use the Bible, translating and learning the language verse by verse.

"But, Madam, this is not good Malayalam. It is not classical Malayalam. It is too common." stated Davidas.

"Do ordinary people understand this Malayalam of the Bible?" I asked.

"Yes," answered Davidas.

"Then that is exactly what I want to learn."

It quickly became evident that I needed other help as well. Learning the language was slow work. I suggested a plan for training deaconesses. Some missionaries saw it as an opportunity for widows and other poor women to realize an income, however small. I managed to recruit five women — three widows and two younger women. We needed quarters for them, so I supervised the building of a house with room for 12 women.

Two missionaries and several Indian pastors were asked to teach classes, which included Bible study, theology and church history. I focused on the practical, teaching them how to conduct meetings or Bible study groups and to visit in the homes. After two years of training, each of the five women was consecrated as a deaconess.

In other areas of our mission, Bible women were trained to go into homes and teach Scripture to the women. In the

Ambur area, Louise Rathke and others had been training and supervising Bible women for years. Missionary wives Pauline Buehner, Gertrude Stelter and others held meetings and helped the women in many ways.

Although I had been told I would be doing *zenana* work (a *zenana* is a room or enclosure in which high caste Brahmin women were kept in strict seclusion), the women I worked with were neither high caste nor secluded. They were very poor. They did not own a Bible and had they owned one they could not have read it. Literacy classes and Bible classes were urgently needed. And there was so much I needed to learn — to fit in, to adjust everything I had learned (even all I was taught in mission school) to a lifestyle and culture so different. I had to learn about Indian women, their customs and their problems. What a culture shock it was when on my first visit to Alleppey, a village about 100 miles up the coast, I was met by a group of women who wore no clothing above the waist! They were older women who worked in the coir industry making ropes and mats.

Christmas in India

I went to Vadakangulam to spend Christmas with Missionary Henry Peckman and his family. Vadakangulam is about 60 miles from Trivandrum and a few miles from the southernmost tip of India. There were a church, a high school and two bungalows on the compound; the Peckmans lived in one and Missionary Arnold Lutz and his family in the other. Christmas Eve I went with Henry Peckman and Arnold Lutz to a village some miles from Vadakangulam. A platform was built in the middle of the village at an intersection. I had to sit up on that platform while Henry and Arnold preached in Tamil. We were given a glass of warm milk, richly flavored. I was afraid to drink it and afraid not to.

Henry and Arnold said, "You have to drink it. They will be offended if you don't."

I do not like milk, especially warm milk flavored with sugar and who knows what else. I decided that the Lord who helped me through teaching all eight grades in Kodaikanal would help me through this glass of milk.

The Lord also helped us when the old touring car got stuck in the sand on our way home. With Arnold driving and Henry and me pushing, we finally got through. But I lost the pretty silk scarf I had tied around my head. It got stuck in a thorn tree while I was pushing. I did not go back for it.

Getting Around

There was no car for me so they gave me a bicycle. Now in India, seeing a woman — a foreigner — on the road was the next thing to a three-ring circus. But a foreign woman on a bicycle was something else again! When I tried to ride over to the other mission compound, the children lined up across the road so that I had to stop. That way they could prolong the fun. To them it was a strange sight, and I'm sure it made their day.

After some new cars arrived from the United States, they gave me a missionary's 13-year-old, beat-up Ford Prefect. Thirteen years on those roads would do any car in! Nothing at all worked on the dash and every once in a while the ignition would shut off for no reason. I had to pump the petrol into the carburetor before it would start. There was a lever near the carburetor that I'd pump up and down and then run back and start the car.

This was the car on which I learned to drive. I was late for my driver's test, having had a flat tire on the way, and my nerves were a complete shambles. I passed anyway. Over the years I received a number of new cars. I had more than 100,000 miles on one car alone. I had to do a lot of driving to get to meetings, classes or to the villages for house visiting.

My first new car was a British Austin. I learned how to clean the battery terminals and to top up the brake and clutch fluids. The roads were bad and shock absorbers had to be replaced often. One day Missionary Paul Schirmer came by and said, "Come on, we're going to buy you a new car." And just like that I had a new Hindustan. I was thrilled.

Traveling long distances by train was exciting too. Although we usually traveled second class, once I went third class. I was in the women's compartment, where women were sitting on the floor. I had a seat but no place to put my feet. I felt my ticket included my feet too, but the women complained and I had a problem. I had some lemonade left in my flask, and after I shared it with the women we got along fine, and they allowed me a little space for my feet.

Susi

Two Indian children greet Susi before Bible stories begin

A woman stopped Susi on the road. "What are you teaching my son?" the woman asked.

"Why?" Susi replied.

"When we have our family *puja* [prayers to the family idols] my son says, 'I will not pray to those gods; I will only pray to Jesus.'"

Susi did not know how to answer, but her heart was filled with joy. Religion could not be taught during school hours, but Susi's pupils liked her Bible stories so much that a large group of young children came to school early each day to hear them. One time Susi was teaching the story of Elijah and the prophets of Baal; the children sat entranced as Susi put each piece of the flannelgraph on the board. When the fire came down from heaven to consume the offering, the children burst into loud applause.

Susi, a dedicated Christian woman and an excellent teacher, was my assistant for many years. The male missionaries each had a "writer," a sort of male secretary. They did odd jobs for the missionary — one of which was waiting long hours in government offices for things that had to be done there. But Susi was much more than a writer. She helped me in so many ways. There were two others before Susi — P. Lois and V. Graceammal, both Indian pastors' daughters — who had left to further their education so they could get better paying work. Susi tried for a long time to get into teacher's training. Finally, with the Lord's help and a little assistance from me, she became a trained teacher. Susi did get a teaching job, but she continued to help me after school, on weekends and during vacations.

Susi and I assembled more than 100 flannelgraph Bible stories. Some I had brought out from the United States and some Susi cut out and colored from sheets of pictures for flannelgraph put out by the Church of South India. To keep the pieces together, I had a portfolio for each lesson and these were stood up, side by side, in a metal cabinet. The board, made of heavy pasteboard covered with flannel, folded in half and had carrying handles. We also had a wooden easel. We never went out without everything we needed for a good Bible lesson. We used the flannelgraph for women's meetings and Bible classes, as well as for the children. Sometimes we stood the easel up on the roadside. With a large group around us, Susi used the pictures to tell the Gospel message.

On Sundays we would leave at 6:00 a.m., drive to Nilemel, a village 30 miles from Trivandrum, and have Bible class for the women before church service. On the way back we stopped at Killiamanoor and had Bible class for the women there. When we got back to Trivandrum it was lunch time, so we had rice and curry in Xavier's restaurant or the hotel, and then it was on to Muloor, 12 miles the other side of Trivandrum, for a 3:00 p.m. Bible class with the women in the church there. We would arrive home around 6:00 p.m. — tired, hot and ready for a bath.

Susi had a wonderful sense of direction. I never had to worry about getting lost when she was in the car. I often wondered why so many churches were off the beaten track — seemingly in the middle of nowhere. I was told that when someone had a small piece of land to donate and wanted a church there, that's where it was built.

One Handful of Rice

One Sunday as Susi and I were leaving the church at Killiamanoor, the pastor and practically the entire congregation followed us to the car. The pastor spoke first, "Mariama, a young wife, is four months pregnant. She fell and is in danger of losing her baby. They are keeping her in the dispensary nearby. She is very poor and her family cannot bring her food." (In India the hospital or dispensary does not provide food for the patients. The food must be brought from home. Very often it is cooked right on the veranda.) "Will you take her in your car to General Hospital in Trivandrum?" the pastor continued.

The trip was almost 30 miles over terrible, unpaved roads. That day I was driving a beat-up old Austin van that made so much noise we were deafened. And it shook us up so much I wondered what it would do to the poor woman. I pointed out the danger to the pastor. "I cannot take Mariama to town in this car; it would surely be dangerous to her in her condition."

"But what can the poor woman do? She will go hungry."

I looked around and saw a rich supply of food growing — rice fields, vegetables and tapioca. I turned to the members. "You know, if each of you took a little rice in one hand and a few vegetables in the other Mariamma would have more than she can eat. In fact you could feed the whole family. You will not miss a little bit of rice and a few vegetables." They learned that day that even though they were very poor, they could feed others. Thus was born a project throughout the Trivandrum District: "For Christmas — A Handful of Rice." The concept was not new; other Lutheran missions had been doing this for the poor in their midst for some time. But I saw a wonderful opportunity for outreach to the community and added another dimension to the project. The handful of rice and a few vegetables were to be collected only from Christian members' homes. At the church volunteers were to fill two-pound plastic bags. A beautiful Christmas card was to be put in each bag so that it showed. The card, outlined in gold, included the Holy Family, the angel's song and John 3:16. The bags were to be delivered only to non-Christian homes where the people were very poor and had little or no food. The Hindus and Muslims could see the love that flows from the hearts of Christians.

In some areas the rice did go to Hindu homes, but in one large city church I was asked to hand out bags of rice to members of the congregation. I felt sad. They had missed the point.

The Wine Bishop

After Ted and Lorene Koepke left India and I was the only missionary in Trivandrum, an Indian man named Frederick worked in the office for me. One of the best jobs he did was to get my accounts out on time — a task that was always difficult for me. He helped deal with the compound workers and made the communion wine for the area. You see, I was the Wine Bishop. Most of the area was dry, and we could only get permission to make wine for communion if I signed the appropriate papers as the Wine Bishop. Pastors had to come to my office to get their wine for Sunday communion. Frederick was also very good at getting matters expedited in government offices, truly a man's job in India.

Teaching at the Seminary

A group of girls had been admitted to the seminary at Nagercoil to train as volunteers for work in their own areas or home churches. The training was later extended so the girls could work as Bible women or take leadership positions among the women of their congregations. The seminary faculty thought it would be good for the girls to have at least one female teacher, someone with whom they could be more comfortable, and asked me to be the one. The class was a mixture of Tamil and Mayalee girls. Every week for six years I made the 42-mile trip to Nagercoil. On the first day I would have class from 8:30 a.m. until noon. Then I had lunch with one of the missionary couples. In the afternoon we had practical training. I would stay overnight in the camp bungalow. Early next morning class would meet until noon, after which I would make my way back to Trivandrum until the following week.

Our studies included teaching methods and techniques, audio-visual aids, how to lead a ladies' aid meeting, how to lead a Bible class or teach Sunday school, and practical training. For the practical portion of visual aids, we practiced making flannelgraph sets from newspaper, magazine pictures or line drawings. Most of the figures had to be cut out and colored. One student colored all the people, even Bible characters, purple — another, pink.

"Is that how you see all the Europeans?" I asked. (Foreigners, whether from America or Europe, are called Europeans.)

"Yes," she replied, and she named a missionary whose complexion was a shade of pink.

A Bible in Every Home

As education expanded in India, usually at least one person in every home could read. I had a fund of 1,000 rupees (at that time around $150). A large number of Bibles had been bought

An Indian woman receives a Bible

for 18 rupees each, and for three rupees the women could take
home a Bible. They loved having their own Bibles.

College Students

"Please Madam, you must come on the retreat so that the
girls will get permission to come," the boys pleaded.
Parents would give permission only if I was there the entire
time to chaperon. So, feeling sorry for the boys, I got involved
in college students' activities. It turned out to be work I really
enjoyed — even when it meant sleeping on a cot without a
mattress or on the floor or out on the veranda. The girls would
not allow a window to be opened, and sleeping eight or ten in
a room with no air was more than I could take.

Missionary Paul Pollex worked with the youth and ensured
that their programs were well thought-out and well executed.
At one youth convention that included college students, some
church officers became angry and physically attacked the
young people. The youth showed unbelievable restraint and
took a lot of physical abuse without defending themselves. I
rescued the girls from harm, taking them to the mission bungalow, and I took one young man to the hospital. I did not go
to bed that night!

When I left India the youth gave me a beautiful inscribed
ivory cross. Most of our college students went on to be teach-

ers and pastors. We knew that the future of our church in India rested on the shoulders of these young people. Our work with them was a special blessing.

A Bible study for college girls

The Plight of Young Girls

According to cultural rules, an Indian girl cannot remain unmarried and make it on her own. Marriage is arranged by the parents. It is serious, even a scandal, if a girl remains unmarried. Girls from poor Christian families often could not be married to Christian men because a Hindu wife with a good dowry proved more attractive to the boy's family. The prospective bride's father has to provide riches along with his daughter — jewelry, land, car or other expensive items. A girl's educational degree or any earning potential could take the place of a dowry. But not all girls are good students and teaching methods are often poor. Getting passing grades became literally a matter of life or death.

A girl came to me one day. "Madam," she begged, "please give me a teaching post in your schools."

"I do not have the authority to appoint anyone to our schools. Besides, you are a Hindu and our teachers must be Christian in order to teach in a Christian school," I explained. "I will be a Christian!" she cried. "I am so much in need of this work."

I understood well what it meant to her. Some desperate girls did take their own lives.

One of our mission girls was very depressed. "My father is arranging a marriage for me. The man is not a Christian. I do not want to marry him. I only want to marry a man from my church. What can I do?" Even pastors sometimes arranged a marriage to a man outside the church. It became important for me to do anything I could to help these young people.

When girls did make it to college, they met with a very real problem. Since independence from Britain, teaching English in schools had become less important, so by the time a student reached college level she had a very poor command of the language. But college professors came from other states with different languages, so English was the language used at the university.

One day a girl showed me a notebook from a college lecture. "Missy, please tell me what the professor said," she begged. She had taken notes in English, but what she wrote made no sense. The poor girl had tried to write down every word the professor said, but she could only get a word now and then. I saw an urgent need here. These girls had to learn how to take lecture notes they could read and understand. The girls had to go back to basic, even first-grade English.

To help these girls and others, I formed classes in several places. In my office, for instance, I had 12 small desks and stools and a blackboard. I held class three days a week for the girls living nearby. When the Hindu girls heard about the class, they filled all 12 seats. One of the girls took Sunday school leaflets I had received from the States. She wanted to distribute them in the office where she worked part time. And this girl was a Hindu.

Most of the girls who came to me for help were non-Christian. I always started with prayer and devotion.

I had a tea party for my students, and once I took them to Cape Comorin — at the southernmost tip of India — where three oceans meet: the Arabian Sea, the Bay of Bengal and the

Indian Ocean. Some evenings you can see the sun set and the moon rise at the same time. The Gandhi Memorial is there and a temple dedicated to the virgin Kumari. We watched men carving huge slabs of granite for a Vivekananda Temple being built on a huge rock offshore — the same type of carving done for temples all over India.

The Slums of Trivandrum

Trivandrum had its slums, with liquor and prostitution rampant. Some of our church members lived there. Some nuns of Mother Theresa's order worked in this area. I was thrilled to make their acquaintance and work with them. Miss Achamma Verghese, a professional church worker for the Syrian (Martomite) Church, was also active in this work. She was responsible for getting me involved in the slums where the need was so great. Alongside the nuns I could work, not only with our own members, but among the Hindus. There was a large shed in the center of the slum where a doctor and some nurses operated a clinic several days each week. For two weeks I used the building for vacation Bible school. To show the Hindus that our Triune God is a God of love, we spent many long hours reaching out to the slum dwellers. This was my childhood dream — to go to a far-away land and tell people of the love of Jesus, how He gave His life on the cross so all could inherit eternal life; to help ease suffering where I could; and to share the love and blessings I had received. God was making my dreams come true!

Helping a Stranger

One evening as I was having supper the phone rang. I had just come home from a class for Sunday school teachers. A Sunday school was being conducted on our compound for Hindu children living along the roadside or in the neighborhood.

The phone call was from the police. An American woman had landed at the airport and was causing a lot of trouble. Apparently she had tried to get a taxi to take her up the coast to Calicut, some 250 miles. Having no success and refusing to take no for an answer, she was causing a real row. She was taken to the police station where, according to the police, she became violent. But according to her, she had been roughed up by the police women. By the time they phoned me to see if I could do anything with her, they had taken her to the Mascot Hotel. She refused to go to a room because she was afraid of being locked in. When I arrived at the hotel everyone was in the lounge — police, spectators and the woman. As usual I was wearing a cross on a chain. As soon as the woman saw the cross she said, "I will go with her."

"Will you let her spend the night at your house?" asked the officers.

I immediately agreed. However the woman was still under arrest and, for my safety, the police insisted that four police women also spend the night in my bungalow. What a night it was! Fortunately the bungalow had an upstairs, so the police women could use that while our special guest took a bedroom downstairs. I made the upstairs guests as comfortable as possible, brought them a cool glass of lime juice and bid them good night.

The woman, however, refused to go to bed; I had to listen to her ranting all night. She had met a young Indian man in the north of India and become engaged. He lived in Calicut and that is where she wanted to go. At midnight we were calling the office of the ambassador in New Delhi. I think we spent more than 100 rupees on phone calls before she was satisfied we had done all we could. A couple of times she wanted to leave, and if I did not do what she wanted, I was as bad as the police.

The woman was to see the police commissioner in the morning. So after giving her breakfast (she ate almost nothing), I took her back to the hotel. On the way I pleaded with her to remain calm if she wanted to be released. "You have to let the police see that you will not cause any more trouble," I said. Apparently she took my advice, because the police commissioner assured me later they had helped her and sent her on her way.

The police were grateful for the help they received from the Lutheran mission. I called the embassy in Madras to report the whole thing. The phone connection was so bad I finally sent a written report. The vice consul was especially happy an American missionary cared for a stranger.

The Venice of South India

A lleppey, a busy little backwater thoroughfare, was called the Venice of South India. A canal ran through the middle of the village with boat after boat, most filled with coconut husks, being loaded and unloaded along the canal. The *go-downs* (storerooms) were filled with merchandise ready for shipping. Rope and mat making was one of the main industries. Women and children did most of the work pulling strands from partially decomposed coconut husks and rolling or twisting them into ropes and door mats. Strands dyed different colors hung in rows from ropes tied between trees. The finished products were taken by boat south to Trivandrum and other cities or north to Cochin for shipping to foreign ports.

Backwaters from Trivandrum to Alleppey

In the backwaters of Alleppey, you could walk across the tops of blue hyacinths. Since the plants were used for fertilizer, they grew profusely — and so did the mosquitoes. While malaria was almost eradicated, elephantiasis was a common sight. It was sad to see so many men and women lumbering along with one or both legs horribly enlarged.

I made the 100-mile trip to Alleppey each month. In the early years the road was so bad I could only average about 16 miles per hour. Later the road was tarred and driving was not so slow. On a typical visit I stayed with missionaries Harold and Evie Heinlein. What wonderful hospitality! In the morning I gathered the women — pastors' and catechists' wives mainly — and drove to Shertelley where we had an all-day workshop. Sessions included practice in leading a Bible class or ladies' meetings and training in other special women's work in the congregation. The Christian wife and mother and her responsibility in the home and in the church were stressed. So much depended upon the women having the courage to show the love of Jesus to their sisters in the faith and, even more so, to the non-Christian women among their families, friends and neighbors. At the end of the day I had a lovely supper with the Heinleins. Sometimes Evie played the piano and we sang. I still remember the spiritual, "Restitution." Early the next morning I returned to Trivandrum via Nilemel, where we held a similar workshop for women.

After the Heinleins were gone, I still made regular visits to Alleppey. Their home had become a "camp" bungalow, so we were able to sleep there. We now had a deaconess working in the area. I went along with her, visiting in the homes of women who were lepers. Their condition was so pitiful. My heart ached for these women as I looked for them in dark, poverty-stricken rooms. I thought about how Jesus healed the lepers, and I prayed with them that Jesus would heal them as well. With medication leprosy can be in remission, but the face, fingers or toes can never be restored to the way they were.

Joys and Sorrows

Margaret, daughter of Pastor Yesudasan, had a serious heart defect, probably caused by rheumatic fever she suffered as a child. This young girl spent many hours near death in the hospital. To relieve her mother, I would often sit with Margaret and talk to her about her Savior and getting well again to serve Him. We would pray together. There were times when she was well enough to be at home. The doctor assured her father that her only hope of full recovery was heart surgery. I urged her father to take her to the American Hospital at Vellore for the surgery, but he was reluctant. He was afraid Margaret could not stand the long train ride, and it

was expensive. Pastor Yesudasan finally agreed to take his daughter on the 600-mile trip. A year-and-a-half ago, when I visited Trivandrum, Margaret came to see me in my hotel. She is well and strong and serving her Lord.

There were many such happy moments, rich with blessing. There were also some tragedies that called for heart-rending prayers. Elizabeth, the daughter of

Rose with a healthy Margaret Yesudasan

P. C. Thomas, was a lovely girl with a beautiful singing voice. Her parents were so protective of her they would not permit her to come to any youth meetings. But there was a 60-year-old music teacher who lived next door, and Elizabeth took singing lessons from him. He took her away to the northern part of Kerala where they were married. In India a runaway marriage or one not arranged by the parents is considered an unforgivable sin. Several years passed. Missionary wife Gertrude Stelter and I felt it was time for at least mother and daughter to see each other again. I drove Mrs. Thomas and Gertrude 100 miles to where Elizabeth lived. Although Elizabeth and her mother were reconciled, Elizabeth could not shake off the deep feeling of guilt, and she became mentally ill. She had children by this time. As her condition worsened, her husband abandoned her and the children, sending Elizabeth back home for her parents to care for.

Mrs. Thomas died suddenly of a stroke, and only the father was left to care for Elizabeth. I stood beside Elizabeth and prayed for her as shock treatment was administered. Elizabeth never recovered. Her ruined life, her burden of guilt, remained to haunt her. In spite of our prayers, her mind never healed.

And how my heart ached for a mother whose daughter had taken her own life! This young woman, Nancy, was the sister of Susi, my assistant. Nancy was a nursing student at Mysore State Hospital. When things became overwhelming for her, she took drugs from the hospital to end her life. I tried to comfort the mother, but there is no grief quite like this. I felt her pain and loss and prayed for the right words to say. I held her in my arms and prayed with her when the van carrying her daughter's body was due to arrive. I assured her that Nancy was now at peace in God's forgiving love. I ached with them, for Susi's family had become like my own.

But there were joyous happenings too. When students finally passed their high school or college exams, they could get paid work. Then came the weddings — huge tents decorated with crepe paper and flowers, gorgeous saris, women and girls with beautiful wreaths of jasmine and other flowers in their hair. A shy bride, never having spent a moment alone with the groom, is now his wife for the rest of her life. And the huge wedding feasts of rice and different curries accompanied by music that could be heard for miles around. The music would go on all night.

Trivandrum District Women's League Executive Committee at work

Women's Organization

I spoke at a women's convention in Madurai, describing the work of the International Lutheran Women's Missionary League (ILWML) in America and discussing plans for a similar organization in India. We organized the women in the Trivandrum district and tried to do the same in the other two districts. Meetings, rallies and conventions were held on the district level. I was Women's Work Coordinator for the whole India Evangelical Lutheran Church (IELC). Twice I programmed a convention for women from all three districts. One convention was held in Madurai, the other in Trivandrum. IELC President Thomas Edward conducted a large women's gathering in Nagercoil.

About 30 women from the Trivandrum area went to the Madurai convention by train. What a wonderful experience for these village women. Some had never been on a train. I could not travel with them but made sure that Susi, my assistant, would take good care of them.

The convention was even more exciting for them than the train ride. The women received packets in their own languages. They wore their badges proudly and participated in all the convention activities: songs, meetings, programs, prayers. They even found time to go shopping and see some of the city.

Not until days later did I learn of a frightening experience the women had. Several ladies left the train at a station to get fresh water from a pump on the station platform. Unknown to them the train pulled out. Such panic! The women on the train were screaming and yelling for the train to wait. Finally someone pulled the chain and the train stopped. The three ladies caught up and got back on the train. All were safe again.

One of the women left behind was Susi, the one I had put in charge to keep all the women safe.

We had high hopes for the women's organization, but there were many obstacles. The most difficult were the language problem and the backwardness of the women. Still, there are younger, better educated women who can take over leadership. The seed has been planted, and God will bring good fruit in His own time.

Vacation Bible School

From the time I sat in education classes at Western Reserve University to when I taught kindergarten, first and second grades at St. John's in Cleveland, Ohio, I was deeply interested in teaching young children. It was not enough for the Indian children to learn or memorize Bible stories; I wanted them to understand how to relate to God's Word to their everyday

Vacation Bible school children singing "Two Little Eyes"

experiences. We were desperately in need of materials for vacation Bible schools. During my last ten years in India, I spent three months of every year (along with my other work) writing, preparing and publishing vacation Bible school materials in the Malayalam language. On a budget of 8,000 rupees ($1,000) lessons were prepared for 10,000 children. Pastor Sushilan and seminarian Stanley Lawrence helped me get the Malayalam absolutely correct. Sets included a lesson for each of the ten days, manuals for the teachers, crafts, badges, songs and games.

I sat for hours at night punching holes in thousands of badges so they could be tied on (pins were not available). We tied hundreds of sets of materials into burlap bags, drove down to the truck depot in the Chalai Bazaar and sent them to churches all over the state of Kerala and into the Peermade Hills. Then came travel to various areas to conduct volunteer training workshops.

Posters advertising our vacation Bible schools were put up everywhere. A large number of Hindu children came to our vacation Bible schools — hundreds throughout all the Lutheran Mission churches. One thing that attracted the children (especially Hindu children) was "dance." Indian children love to dance, and the most serious hymns were often set to a dance step.

I spent the hot season attending a vacation Bible school somewhere. I often had to pick up the teachers to be sure to get them there on time. But that was not all. I had to go to as many closing programs as possible. One of my jobs, which I did not like very much, was to hand out the prizes. Only a few earned prizes, and the rest just sat there and looked on enviously. But I made certain that every child received a gift — a plastic tumbler, a little comb or a pencil and, of course, a certificate signed by the teacher, pastor or superintendent. The smile and the happy look on those little faces as they came forward to accept the gifts and certificates was, I believe, one of the richest blessings God has granted me in my lifetime. A smiling Indian child is beautiful beyond words.

In the Community

I joined the Trivandrum Women's Club, where I met a number of educated Christian women of the Syrian Christian Caste. Hindu and Muslim women, including those of the royal family, were also members. I was asked to decorate the Christmas tree each year. Sitting next to the princess at one Christmas party, I had the opportunity to tell her about the birth of our Savior and what it means to all Christians. Now and then I received a note from the young princess asking me to come to lunch at the palace while we discussed meeting plans.

I was also a member of the India University Women's Association. For their Women's Day observance, I was asked to read a paper on "Women of the New Testament." One of the members was Jewish, and her paper was on "Women of the Old Testament Scriptures." I was surprised to learn that Esther is not found in the Jewish Scripture but is rather a part of Jewish history.

I had many invitations to garden parties at the palace where I met Prime Minister Nehru and his daughter Indira Gandhi and her two small sons. I also received a few invitations to the governor's mansion for a garden party or an "at home" — when the governor and his wife are "at home" to receive you. You hire a driver, arrive at the mansion and step graciously out of the car and into the governor's home. When it is time to leave, the driver brings the car and you step graciously into the back seat and leave — graciously.

I was often invited to the home of the Otwells for Thanksgiving or Fourth of July. The Otwells worked for the United States Information Service. Sometimes I was invited to meet the American ambassador. One hot season I was the only American left on the plains. Everyone else was in Kodaikanal. I was asked to stand with the city officials to meet Eleanor Roosevelt as she came off the plane in Trivandrum. I was introduced to her, she shook my hand, and that was that.

Once when the American ambassador was visiting in Trivandrum there was a problem. The man was almost seven feet tall, and there was no bed in the hotel long enough for him. The city officials called me and asked if I had a long bed. All my beds were the standard six feet, I told them, but I suggested they use a bed without a foot board and add a large square coffee table or footstool. I don't know what they finally did, but I guess it worked out all right.

The ambassador always liked to spend his vacation at Kovalam, the world-famous beach on the Arabian Sea. People came from all over the world to spend hours in this beautiful cove. When I lived in the village of Balaramapuram, I was only four miles as the crow flies from Kovalam. When I moved back into Trivandrum, I was only eight miles away.

When Dr. O. H. Schmidt, LCMS Director of Foreign Missions, came from the United States to visit, he spent a day-and-a-half with each missionary. The idea was that we should show him our work. By the time he came to see me, he had been through the mill.

"Dr. Schmidt, what would you like to do?" I asked.

"Miss Ziemke," he replied. "I would like to go swimming at Kovalam beach and see an Indian movie."

So that is what we did. I did take him one morning with a deaconess to visit some homes.

Dr. Florence Montz and Dr. Robert Zimmer came on a fact-finding tour for Wheat Ridge Ministries, an organization that funds Christian health care work around the world. After lunch at my house, I took them to Balaramapuram, where the people in the area wanted to use a bungalow for a dispensary. From there I took them to beautiful Kovalam beach.

"What Was Hard for You?"

"What was hard for you when you were in India?" I was asked recently. I had to stop and think. First, seeing so much pain and suffering. I remember the first time I was taken to visit a home. A woman was lying on a dirt floor in a dark room. When she turned toward me, I saw that half her face was eaten away with cancer. That was more than 40 years ago. The government has made a lot of progress since then in helping the sick and suffering, but there is still so much to do.

Second, I love animals. While I felt deep sympathy for the hungry people and did all I could to help, I also felt pain for the helpless, starving animals.

Third, I learned how it feels to be single in a family- or couple-oriented environment, to have no one to share your frustrations or setbacks. Sometimes I felt like exploding. Prayer, of course, always helped. God supplied two missionaries, Pastor Gerhardt Stelter and Pastor Andrew Buehner, as friends. They just listened, which helped so much. And I did find peace and joy in my work. But I felt the loneliness most when I saw something breathtakingly beautiful. I remember walking my dog around the compound on a beautiful night — there is nothing so beautiful as a tropical moonlit night. I needed someone to share it with me, but no one was there.

Finally, in India there was a constant battle with insects. Roaches are everywhere! Brown ones, pink ones, blue ones, green ones, purple ones — walking, flying, in the book cases, in the closets! And tiny lizards that managed to drop their tails in your soup. Ants of every color — red fire ants whose bite was as bad as a bee sting, white ants (termites) destroying everything in their path. They built bridges from a crack in the wall to the table where your books were lying. Then there were huge spiders, scorpions and deadly snakes. Once a scorpion fell out of the ceiling and landed on my shoulder. I felt a little like St. Paul as a friend brushed it off. One day I saw a cobra on my back porch with its hood fanned out, spitting at my dog, who was keeping a safe distance. And finally rats, like the one scrabbling at my back and toes one night in bed. Earlier in my life, if I ever thought about anything like that happening, I was sure I would die. Well, I did not die. Next morning I hardly thought about it, but we did set a trap!

Children present a play for World Sunday School Day

To India and Back

I returned to the United Stated in September of 1978. I could have gone back to India for another year, but IELC President Thomas Edward wanted me to move to Madras to plan and head an IELC women's organization similar to the ILWML. I would have had to start all over again with only ten months to get off the ground. I could not accomplish enough in that time to warrant so much expense — travel, salary, housing, car, etc. In the light of good stewardship, I decided not to go back. So with a sad heart that misses India so much, I will spend the rest of my days in the United States.

Yet I am thankful that God called me and allowed me to be a deaconess in the beautiful land of India. Yes, India is beautiful even though it has its ugliness, its poverty, its sickness and suffering. The beauty is in God's creation and in the people, especially the children.

I am amazed as I think back on the path that led me to India. Although I came from an unchurched home, I was baptized at the age of six and my mother, not a believer herself, sent me to Sunday school. It just happened to be Lutheran and a deaconess was my Sunday school teacher. We later moved, and my mother allowed me to attend confirmation class at Immanuel Lutheran Church in Pittsburgh, Pennsylvania. I was confirmed there two years later. My mother died when I was almost 15 and Immanuel became a haven for me. I was active in the Walther League youth program and taught Sunday school. I always remembered the deaconess and always I wanted to be one too. I dreamed of going to a far country to tell about the love of Jesus. I know the Lord has chosen me, called me and led me.

In November 1993 I received a wonderful gift: a return trip to Trivandrum, India. The Sunday after we arrived was World Sunday School Day. A special program was planned, and again I had the joy of looking into the beautiful smiling faces of the children.

Another day the women of the area gathered for a special meeting. The girls now had become wives, mothers, teachers or office workers. We met in what was the conference hall but is now Concordia Church. The women got up and spoke about the work I had done with them, the training I had given them and, most wonderful of all, assured me they were still serving their Lord. Then we all received a candle. Silence fell as we carefully lighted them and stood in a circle. We raised our candles high and sang: "This little Gospel light of mine, I'm going to let it shine!" We felt such joy in the love of Jesus and the love of each other. We took pictures and hugged and smiled. And I think we all cried a little. I know I did.

Rose and friends singing "This Little Gospel Light of Mine"

The Beauty That Is India
by Rose Ziemke

The beauty that is India:
The darkness, the light,
The glory that is past,
The redeeming that is now.

The sadness, the joy
The life, the death,
The songs and the stillness,
The beauty that always will be!

The beauty that is India:
The children, the youth,
The future that is India:
The families that love.

The pain, the suffering,
The hunger, the struggle without end.
Weep now
For the beauty that is India!

Drying my tears
I pray for the souls,
Remembering
The beauty that is India!

Rose Ziemke served as a deaconess in India for more than 30 years. She retired to St. Louis, Missouri, where she works part-time in the LCMS Mission Department.

Mary Esther's Mission

by Ruby Young

Henry and Mary Esther Otten were sent to India by The Lutheran Church–Missouri Synod (LCMS) to work among the Muslims. Many thought it an impossible dream. While in India they wrote regularly to their friends back home, giving personal perspective and insight into their field of service. These letters also tell the story of Mary Esther's mission, which she pursued her whole life long: bringing the gospel of Jesus Christ to the Muslims. Excerpts of these letters follow.

Mary Esther shortly before her marriage

Beginnings

Dear friends,

This is the first missionary letter we are sending to our friends at home. Our prayer is that God will bless these messages and use them to knit us together in a bond of fellowship and common interest in His Gospel.

Thursday, March 30, 1950 was the day we had been waiting for — sailing day. Our cousin, Mrs. Herman Otten, came to see us off as the representative of the Lutheran Women's Missionary League (LWML). We had expected our departure to be a dramatic moment, an hour of destiny. None of these thoughts entered our minds. Passing the Statue of Liberty seemed more like seeing it from the Staten Island ferry than being on a freighter bound for India.

When we awoke next morning, we were on the open sea! It was not long before we felt the ship lifting and dipping with the swells. We felt our stomachs lift and dip too! We lost only one meal each, but whenever the sea was rough we felt better lying in our bunks or sitting on deck chairs. Once we entered the Mediterranean Sea our spirits soared. The water was much calmer than the Atlantic, and we saw land of some sort almost every day. We also saw our first porpoises, the friendly fish that enjoy racing with the prow of the ship.

A month after leaving the United States, we arrived in Bombay and received our first impressions of India. We later found that some of these were not a true picture of India. We spent three days in Bombay and visited two particular places of interest — the Hanging Gardens and the Parsi Towers of Silence. The Hanging Gardens consisted of neatly trimmed lawns, hedges and pathways with flowered shrubs and plants scattered about. Despite the fine sounding name, the Parsi Towers were a gruesome spectacle. A tower of silence is a place for the disposal of dead bodies. The Parsis dispose of their dead by laying the bodies within these large circular walls and letting vultures eat them.

On May 3 we landed at Madras and spent the next three days trying to get our goods through customs. As soon as we had taken care of our baggage, we flew to Trivandrum in the southern tip of India. The missionaries there wanted to meet us and give us some tips about housekeeping in India before we went to our own field further north. At Nagercoil we attended an Indian church service, held in the Malayalam tongue, the language we are now studying. It was an inspiration to hear Christian hymns in language and melodies strange to us and yet feel the bond of fellowship that made us all one in Christ.

The next day we started north toward our own field of service. An Austin car had been procured for us. We wanted to drive it ourselves, but it was a good thing we were persuaded to hire a native driver. Driving an auto in India is a far cry from driving one in America. Traffic moves on the left, the driver's seat is on the right and the roads are not marked in many places. The roads are not primarily for autos but for pedestrians, bicycles, bullock carts, cows, goats, chickens, dogs, cats and water buffalo. All these have the right-of-way over an auto.

The first day we drove from Trivandrum to Alleppey, about 100 miles right up the coast. The next afternoon we arrived at our destination, Calicut. It was with a great deal of joy that we met Dr. Henry Nau, the man who had initiated the interest in Muslim missions and would now aid us in getting started.

Our home is not right in Calicut but in a town called Feroke about six miles away. We have learned how to exist in India. That is not so simple. Meals are a real problem; there is no A&P grocery just around the corner. Canned goods are scarce, and some articles such as flour, sugar, bread, rice and gasoline are rationed.

We have engaged a language teacher and meet with him every weekday for several hours. We have been able to make some tours further inland and look over the towns where we might take up work later on. Our work here on the Malabar Coast will be done especially among a Muslim people know as the Moplahs. Moplah men can be identified by their shaven heads. Moplah women do not wear the veil but are often seen with an umbrella.

Our travels are over now, and ahead lies the work for which we came. We covet your prayers and ask that God prepare our tongues and spirits for the task that lies ahead.

The First Decade

1950

Perhaps the first thing that will strike your eye is our change of address. Three months ago our landlord told us his house in Calicut had been sold and his family needed our house. We found a new house in Calicut and moved in, which was quite a chore. In India there are no moving companies with nice covered, padded trucks. We hired a truck from an Indian ex-servicemen's company and engaged some coolies from a local coolie boss. The coolies do not have much of an appreciation for fine things, and if you don't watch them you are liable to find your furniture all scratched, your kerosene refrigerator ruined and perhaps some items missing. So we just let them do the heavy carrying and carried a lot of the stuff ourselves. Many of the Indians consider common labor degrading, and it is somewhat of a rarity to see an educated man carrying a load, even groceries or his own suitcase. More and more we have learned to appreciate the Christian emphasis on the dignity of labor. We are taking every opportunity to tell by word and example that all work is honorable before God as long as it is honest labor.

Our new home is located right in the city about two-and-a-half blocks from the ocean. Down to the ocean makes a nice walk. We miss the quietness and fresh air we had in Feroke, but we are closer to the Indian people in our present home. That is important both for learning the language and for getting to know them. Our language work is going on day by day. Almost all missionaries spend at least a year studying the language. We can carry on simple conversation now and have a pretty good idea of the structure of the language.

Running a household here takes much longer than in the States, and the climate is so energy-sapping that a woman would soon be worn to a shred if she tried to do all the work herself; servants are a necessity. Missionary homes in India are much larger than parsonages in the States. The large rooms provide the necessary air and coolness needed in the hot weather, and since there are very few hotels in India for westerners, the missionary home also serves as a guest house. Rice is the main food of the Indians in this area. The principal food preparation is rice and curry. There are many kinds of curry. Some are made of vegetables, others of meat, others of fish, etc. We have become accustomed to the spices, and if we don't have any rice and curry for a few days we get hungry for it.

None of the more serious illnesses such as malaria or dysentery have bothered us yet. Now that we are living in town with much filth and trash lying about, we shall be in more danger. We have the downstairs screened in. At night we sleep under mosquito net.

In June we traveled to Ponnani with Dr. Nau. At Tirur we left the car at the police station and boarded a bus. These Indian buses are really a sight to behold! They hold an endless number of people and most everyone has one or two packages. We rode six or seven miles when all at once we stopped. The driver opened one of the doors and motioned for us to get out. There we saw in front of us not a road but water. Everyone was piling into two small boats that carried us across the water to the road on the other side. When we got to the other side the boats could not pull clear up to the shore. That did not trouble the Indians; they were barefooted and waded to shore. They put a bench into the water for us and we walked first on that, but it was not long enough so we, too, waded to shore. Dr. Nau rode piggy-back on one of the Indian boatmen. Another bus was waiting to take us into Ponnani.

As we walked down the street in Ponnani, a crowd started forming immediately. You would have thought we ran an orphanage and were taking the children for a walk. We started for the mosque, the Muslims' place of worship. We came past one wing of the building in which there was only a large pool of water with several smaller ones around the side. These are for performing ablutions before a Muslim can enter the mosque. Dr. Nau offered to take off his shoes upon entering the mosque but was told that we could not go in at all. We decided to go back to Tirur by boat. Just like every other public conveyance in India, the boat will let you off wherever you want. Sometimes there is no dock, so we got as close to shore as possible and the men folded their skirts and waded ashore. Back at Tirur we got our car from the police station.

Dr. Nau left us at the beginning of August. We were thankful that he had been here to help us get started and glad to hear that God granted him a safe journey home. Now we were on our own.

We went down to Trivandrum the first part of August for a conference. The Lutheran Mission in India is divided into three districts: Trivandrum, Nagercoil and Ambur. The Tamil language is used in the Nagercoil and Ambur districts and the Malayalam language in the Trivandrum district.

We may spend Christmas with the missionaries in Alleppey. No doubt it will seem odd to celebrate Christmas in warm weather. When we think of the Muslim faith, we can only think of a dead prophet and dead letters in a book. How wonderful it is to have a loving, living Savior in such a time as this!

1951

We began the New Year with a new language teacher. In February it began to get hot and by the end of March we were glad the time for hill leave had arrived. The mission owns a number of bungalows at a hill station called Kodaikanal. Kodaikanal is about 7,000 feet above sea level and has a nice cool climate. Children of the missionaries attend school there.

On June 16th our home was blessed with the advent of David Michael, 7 pounds, 2 ounces. He has added much joy to our home. We think that he may be a help to us in our work. There is something about the magnetic smile of a small child that seems to melt barriers. Among the women especially there is a great interest in the "white baby."

In October we moved from Calicut to Wandoor, about 42 miles east of Calicut and resting in the shadows of the Western Chat mountains. It is in the heart of the Muslim population of Malabar, a virgin mission field with not a single Christian church in 500 square miles. We found people who did not even know what a missionary was!

Soon after we came here we decided to plant a garden. That turned out to be much more of a job than we thought. We forgot to reckon with the stray goats and cows that daily invade the compound. The first task then was not spading but making a fence. So far we have planted radishes, onions, okra, eggplant and tomatoes. We are looking forward to the tomatoes most of all.

1952

Opening a dispensary in Wandoor has been our main project during the last six months. Dr. Mary Abraham will be in charge. Dr. Abraham is still very young, but her Christian outlook and willingness to make the best of sometimes primitive conditions have proved a valuable asset to the dispensary, which opened on April 3rd and is called Karunalaya Dispensary — Karunalaya means "Abode of Mercy."

Although it is the rainy season, the sun is shining brightly. It's a day that would promote spring fever in America. But conditions in the world are far different from the quiet beauty surrounding us; unrest in the world is a constant reminder of the words, "Work while it is day, ere the night cometh when no man can work." One of the urgencies in mission work is to get Indian Christians interested in spreading the Gospel. Recently one young Muslim man, with tears in his eyes, expressed doubts about his faith. Why does he not become Christian? The answer is given in two words: "Rama Sinham." Rama Sinham was a Muslim who lived about 20 miles from Wandoor and became a Hindu because of a dream. The Muslims murdered him. The murderers were known but never convicted; there is ugly talk about bribery. The shadow of Rama Sinham hangs all over the west coast of India. We consider it one of our main tasks to inspire and encourage our Indian coworkers to recognize the call to work among Muslims.

Last month we purchased eight acres of land a half-mile from the center of town for a new dispensary. This new location will afford a healthier place in which to work and live since it is located on a hill and will be well supplied with refreshing breezes. We hope to complete the construction of the dispensary, the doctor's house and our bungalow before the next rainy season.

God has blessed us with good health. Little David is full of life and looks sturdy. When Hank was examined in St. Louis before we came here, the doctors discovered a heart weakness. The doctor asked him, "Do you really want to go to the mission field?" Hank said, "Yes." Out of three years in India, he has been sick only one day.

1953

The greatest event in our personal lives since we last wrote was the birth of our daughter, Miriam Sue, on August 23. We thank the Lord that He gave us another healthy child. Our hearts were also gladdened by the arrival of Roland and Mary Helen Miller, who will be our coworkers among the Muslims here in Malabar.

The first project for constructing the new dispensary was digging the well. The hand of the Lord was evidently with us; people had grave doubts as to whether we would find water on the land. The property is surrounded by granite rock on four sides. We were told about a water diviner who had quite a reputation, so we sent for him. His tests were tried on a number of places, but only one registered positive. Rev. David, our

Indian coworker, supervised the digging. When the work started, the local people were quick to say we did not have much chance of striking water before striking rock. Rev. David told them we had the same God Moses had. If that God could make water come out of a rock for Moses, He could do the same for us. As the hole grew deeper, Rev. David explained some Bible stories to the men who were digging. In the end his bold faith was rewarded. We struck water at only 23 feet and were not at all bothered with rock.

Now that the rainy season is over we can go out with our Bible slides and flannelgraph board. Just before sunset is best for flannelgraph and just after sunset for showing slides.

We need a battery for showing slides so have to stay within reach of a car. But the flannelgraph kit is light, and with it we walk into more interior places. We start with a song. As soon as people hear us singing they come to see why. When a good group has gathered around we present our message, explaining a story with pictures. Afterward we invite the people to look at our books and take some tracts. The people listen attentively and are willing to have us come back.

We also go to the weekly markets and sell books. The Bible Society has put out a Gospel of Matthew in Arabic-Malayalam (Arabic letters but Malayalam words). The society has just finished printing the Gospel of Luke. In addition to actual selling, we do quite a bit of talking about the books. When someone shows interest in a picture, it gives us an opportunity to explain the story and bring home some truth about Christ.

1954

Since the land we purchased for the dispensary is almost eight acres and Rev. David found it difficult to let the rich land lie idle, we now have a field of rice surrounding our new buildings. We hope to get back our investment and in future years give surplus rice for the alleviation of famine or some other helpful project.

Hank and Mary Esther with David and Miriam

In June the second Indian pastor who will work among the Muslims was ordained. He is Rev. Challeyyan, a recent graduate of the Lutheran seminary in Nagercoil.

Before we went on our vacation, we received ten barrels of milk powder for famine relief. We gave one to another missionary for distribution in his area and then began distribution among the needy here. We mixed up a certain amount every day and gave a large cupful to each child who came. We gave more than 100 children a cup of milk daily. Now more children are coming. We can see visible improvement in the health of some of the children.

Through our distribution of milk, we have become acquainted with many Muslim women. They are eager to invite us in to their homes. We go laden with our flannelgraph materials and some newly printed Malayalam Sunday school lessons. With the continual arrival of new babies in every household, we have a good reason to visit. They love to hear us sing and seem fascinated that Mary Esther sings Malayalam lyrics. Many Muslims think Christians believe about as Muslims do. This attitude is more difficult to combat, humanly speaking, than people who have no knowledge of Jesus at all.

We have moved into our new home, and it is such a joy to be here. It seems impossible that one's surroundings could make such a difference, but it is true. From the upstairs of the former home, we would look out and see mostly trees and brush. Now we are situated on the top of a hill. On two sides we see mountains that make up part of the Nilgiris range. It is a thrill to see the sun go down — the sky fills with a maze of orange and red colors turning deep red and purple as the sun sinks below the green rice field.

Miriam is 26 months old. She runs all over and is learning to talk. David loves to play with other children. Our cook has two boys, and the three of them have a wonderful time together.

1955

The work here has witnessed a number of changes since the first of the year. Dr. Mary Abraham, the Indian doctor who has been with us from the beginning, took a post at another hospital. We were without a doctor for a month, then succeeded in obtaining the services of Dr. Saranrna Thomas from the middle of March until the latter part of June. Dr. Thomas had four years of medical experience, and the number of patients doubled. The arrival of Dr. Thomas was a gift of God to our work.

One case stands out in particular, a man of about 55 suffering from double pneumonia. By the time we got to his house, he looked as if he were breathing his last. We concluded it was too late to pray for him. Dr. Thomas asked the man's son to hold his arm while she administered an injection to stimulate his heart. The son refused, saying there was no use hurting the poor old man in his last moments. Dr. Thomas gave the shot anyway, followed by penicillin. We told the son to come next morning and report on his father's condition, little thinking he could live through the night. As a rebuke to our weak faith, the son came early the next morning and said his father was much better. After that many patients came from that area. We felt ashamed for having doubted the ability of God. We were sorry when Dr. Thomas left, but once again the Lord supplied. Dr. Annamma Isaac has come, and we hope she will stay for quite a while.

From the time we came to Wandoor, a Muslim man named Ahmadkutty had been reading Christian books in our reading room and discussing various parts of them with Rev. David. Now we have been privileged to see the Word of God take root; Ahmadkutty was baptized in January. As a Christian he could hardly expect to get work in Wandoor, so he went to a mountainous area where he had spent some of his early years. There he found a job on a tea estate as washerman and day laborer. The Muslim equivalent of the FBI sent word to the Muslims on the estate that Ahmadkutty was a Christian. When they threatened to reconvert him to Islam, he ran away. Please pray for him. His Christian name is Paul.

Recently a Muslim religious teacher told the school children, under the threat of punishment, that they should not come to our reading room because the books and pictures there would cause them to err from the faith (Islam). For a few days there were very few pupils in the reading room, but then they started coming back again. Opposition like this is encouraging in some ways because it shows the Word of God is having some effect.

1957

It has been a long time since we wrote and perhaps some of you are wondering if we are still on the mission field. The answer is yes — all five of us. James Martyn joined David and Miriam on June 15, 1956. Then we were on furlough in America from September 1956 until October of this year.

When we returned to India, a bus took us from Calicut to Wandoor. As we neared the mission driveway, the driver suddenly began honking the horn loudly and continuously. Just then we looked up the road and saw a crowd of people waiting to welcome us. After traveling half-way around the world by car, ship, plane, train and bus, how glad we felt to see several hundred local people, mostly Muslims, welcoming us home.

Remember we told you about Ahmadkutty, the new Christian who was persecuted after his conversion? In addition to being threatened and given promises of aid by his former Muslim friends, the Christians were suspicious of him and did not receive him with full confidence. Faced with all this, he went back to his old religion. This event taught us that our task does not only involve preaching to Muslims but also encouraging and helping the Indian church to become a home for converts.

1958

One of the big changes during the last six month is that the administration of the mission has passed from the hands of the missionaries into the hands of the India Evangelical Lutheran Church (IELC), where it rightly belongs. One of the lessons learned from mission history in China is that the local Christians should learn to take responsibility for their own church affairs as soon as possible. Usually this includes self-government, self-propagation, self-support. The necessary start has been made, and the church in India needs prayer to meet the challenge.

In Wandoor we have had some heartening experiences with the distribution of Christian literature. We have a new Jeep station wagon and thought, "Why not use the tailgate for our literature?" This put the items for sale closer to eye level and immediately drew a more interested audience. Rev. David used a loud-speaker to describe some of the books on display. Then the rest of us circulated in the crowd with a display in our hands. If a person showed some interest, we tried to place a book in his hands for inspection. Some accepted the books gladly; others looked at them and returned them in a polite way; a few refused the books with disdain and spat on the ground. We just smiled and passed on to the next person. From January until the middle of May, we "sold" 3,012 books. The price paid is only a fraction of the actual cost of printing and paper.

Mary Esther has started a private lending library. After purchasing most of the good Christian books available in the Malayalam language, she invited friends and neighbors to take the books home and read them. Kunyalen, a former tuberculosis patient, still comes regularly to the dispensary for medicines. He always stops over at the bungalow to take away some new book from Mary Esther's library. When you see the happiness on his face, you know the Spirit is at work.

A little more than a month ago we were called to a delivery case. When we reached the cluster of huts where we expected to find the woman, she was not there. She came from a Hindu caste that does not permit births to take place inside the house. The people pointed to the woods, and there we saw the woman standing in the forest supported by two other women. We saw a rope hanging from a tree to which the woman could cling for support. There was also a mat on one side for protection and some ashes from a fire that had burned during the night. After three sleepless nights and days, the woman looked haggard and at the point of death. The doctor was forced to examine her right out under the trees. The women of the neighborhood formed a circle around the woman and so created a measure of privacy. Dr. Chacko said the only way the woman could possibly live would be to deliver the baby by caesarean section. We took the patient to the government hospital some 18 miles away. The doctor invited Hank to witness the operation. While Hank prayed, the doctor and his assistants worked; no blood for transfusion, no oxygen for the patient, only some intravenous saline. But God was there. The woman survived.

Now a few words of personal note: David is seven, Miriam is almost five and Jimmy is two. Mary Esther has been teaching David first grade material at home this year. In January he will be going away to school in Kodaikanal with the other missionary children.

1959

The most significant thing that happened to us as a family was the birth of Joel Stephen on May 27. Miriam was hoping strongly for a baby sister but has discovered that baby boys are nice also. Mary Esther is also doing well, and we thank God for His care.

Early in the year we started some new work with Bible correspondence courses. We translated an English course on the Gospel of Mark into Malayalam and had it printed. It is called "Kingdom of God." We decided to concentrate on the "camp" method followed by some other missionaries in the eastern part of India. Instead of sending out the course by post, it is given out personally in a chosen center over a limited period of time. People are invited to start the course by buying the Gospel and at the same time obtaining the first few lessons of the course. They study the lessons at home and bring them to the center for correction. This gives a chance for personal consultation with the evangelists in charge of the center. Upon completion of the lessons, the student receives a certificate plus one or two books about Christ and salvation.

The first center we chose was Nilambur, eight miles north of Wandoor. More than 200 bought the Gospel and took home the first lessons. More than 100 finally completed all the lessons and earned a certificate. Most of these were Hindus and Christians, but there were also a few Muslims.

One good feature of this type of program is that it gets the Muslim to study the Bible with the idea of finding out what it says. To answer the questions, they have to try to discover the meaning. Often Muslims read the Scriptures to find fault with them. If we can get them to approach the Bible from a positive viewpoint, the advantage is obvious. Please remember the work among Muslims in your prayers.

The Otten family: Hank, Miriam, Jimmy, David, Mary Esther and Joel

The Second Decade

1960

When we last wrote, our state of Kerala was in a condition of turmoil and unrest because of impending elections. In February the non-Communist coalition obtained the majority of voters and formed a government. The atmosphere for religious witness is much more favorable. This morning two Muslims were in our worship service. One of them is the young man who helped us write the Bible correspondence course on Mark. He, his wife and three children live on about $8 a month. If he and his family should decide to be baptized, they would likely be evicted from their home, which is on the property of the local Muslim mosque.

Several years ago we were able to help P. Mohammed undergo a heart operation at the mission hospital in Vellore. Sometimes the Muslims threaten him for showing interest in Christianity, but he tells, "I have already died once, and I am not afraid to die again." This kind of courage put a stop to some of the criticism.

The community is starting a nursery school in Wandoor, and Mary Esther is on the committee for conducting the school. A Christian lady from town is going to be the teacher. The opening is set for August 15, India's Independence Day.

When we last wrote we mentioned that all the children were home. Now the house is much quieter. David went back to school in January, and Miriam started school in May. So only Jimmy and Joel are at home now.

1961

On February 12th we had the joy of dedicating our new chapel in Wandoor. Up until now we have been worshipping in one of the rooms of the dispensary, which also served as a reading room during the week. The walls on the side of the chancel are shaped in the form of scrolls as a symbol that the words spoken from the altar and lectern are the Word of God.

Another joy was the Mission Board's approval of our request to expand the dispensary into a 60-bed hospital with a missionary doctor in charge. The medical and evangelistic needs of our area are too much for us to carry on alone.

We have heard of another Muslim convert called Kabir. After his baptism in Bombay, he faced unemployment and came to Bangalore (largest city in South India) looking for work. He could find nothing. He was alone and prayed daily for two weeks for work. Then he spent a whole night in prayer. At 6:00 a.m. he saw a newspaper advertisement in which a dry cleaning establishment gave notice of an opening. Immediately Kabir went to this place. He got there at 6:30 a.m. only to find 22 others had arrived before him. But he stood around with the others until the owner came at 9:00 a.m. Without even speaking to any of the others, the owner immediately pointed to Kabir and said, "I give this work to you."

1962

Miss Velma Math, missionary nurse, came to Wandoor at the end of September 1961 and began a program of language study and medical assistance. Velma stayed in the bungalow with us until her own quarters were completed. As she dashes around the compound from one task to another, we wonder if we have become old or if we need a furlough.

In December Mr. and Mrs. Charles McCreary, both medical doctors, arrived in India to work in Wandoor. This followed the decision of the LWML to include our dispensary expansion as one of their mission projects. When the work is completed, we will have a modern outpatient department with x-ray and laboratory facilities as well as some beds for the general and tuberculosis patients.

We had visions of getting some mission builders, but the Indian government is not favorable to the idea. When we asked a government officer about the possibility of getting a visa for foreign builders he replied: "We built the Taj Mahal. Why do we need foreign builders?" We had no answer to that one.

During the past months we have been conducting services for a group of "diaspora" Christians who have moved to a place about eight miles from Wandoor. They were members of our church in the south and have come up here to farm. We usually go several Sunday afternoons a month and conduct the worship on the veranda of one of the homes. The people sit on reed mats on the floor. The place is somewhat difficult to reach because of a sizable river nearby. Sometimes we wade through the river; other times there is a boat poled by a ferryman. We have found that bare feet are the best way to navigate in mud.

One of the fine Muslim girls who had been working in the nursery school at Malappuram became insane. There is good reason to believe part of her illness is caused by the frustration of being drawn to Christ inwardly but being unable to express her faith outwardly. The last we heard was that her family had her chained up in a small dark room. This morning Velma Math and Mary Helen Miller are taking her to the Mental Health Center of the Christian Medical College Hospital, where we hope she may recover.

1963

We are in the United States for our second furlough, which extends from May 1963 to May 1964. We spent the summer with Hank's folks in Iowa and now are with Mary Esther's mother in Columbus.

The dedication of the expansion of our dispensary was held on May 15, one week before we left. Dr. McCreary and his family are taking up residence in our bungalow. So one family was moving in one side of the house while another was moving out.

In our last letter we wrote about the Muslim young woman at Malappuram who became insane and was being taken to the Christian Medical College Hospital. We are happy to report that she recovered and is now serving again as a helper in the nursery school. Her problem still remains, and we ask you to pray for her.

We had a wonderful trip home. The best part was leaving Kobe, Japan. A brass band was blaring, people were shouting, waving and drinking, but there was another sound. A group of Japanese Christians was standing dockside and singing hymns as a farewell to missionaries who had labored among them. The music of those hymns, sung quietly and hopefully, drifted across the harbor when other sounds had ceased. We thought this was a foretaste of heaven, the final day when people from all countries and climes, all types and tongues, will sing the praise of Him who delivered them from sin and darkness, gave them hope and joy, provided pardon and power — the Lord Jesus Christ.

1965

It doesn't seem possible, but it is already more than a year since we returned from our last furlough. Our children have just started another year of school, and this time our youngest, Joel, has joined his older brothers and sister in going off to school. David is now a student at High Clerc, an American-type high school especially for missionary children located just across the road from our elementary school and boarding home. Miriam is in sixth grade and Jimmy in fourth.

The pharmacist at the hospital, P. J. Varughese, goes to the outlying towns around Wandoor twice a week and administers medicines to tuberculosis patients. This affords a good opportunity for a concentrated witness. We started with a planned distribution of tracts. Various denominations interested in Christian witness to Muslims have pooled their resources and produced a set of tracts with attractive covers and excellent content. The next part of the effort was to invite those who had received tracts to enroll in a Bible correspondence course. Some of the patients have completed three courses.

1966

Would you like to tour to some of the stations in our area? To the south there are two places called Srikrishnapuram and Cherpalcheri. When you see Rev. Victor at his desk preparing Sunday school and Bible correspondence course lessons, you know that Christ has planted His church in India and that it will continue even if all outside help is taken away.

About 20 miles northwest is Malappuram, a center of the Muslim community. Rev. Roland and Mary Helen Miller and their coworkers have been sowing the seed of God's Word here since 1954. In March we were privileged to attend the closing session of the nursery school at Malappuram and were surprised to see the number of Muslim parents who came to see their little children sing Christian songs and act out Bible stories.

Another 30 miles along the main road takes us to Calicut, the largest city in our area, located on the coast of the Arabian Sea. In April and May, the missionaries rented a stall at the municipal exhibition and set up a display with stacks of Bibles, Christian booklets and tracts. Even though the stall was next to a sideshow featuring a "body with two heads," large numbers of people showed interest and purchased literally thousands of pieces of literature.

Fifty miles north and several thousand feet high is Wynaad, our mission field on a plateau where there are now five organized congregations and several preaching stations. This work is mostly among Hindus. One of the most interesting places is Kurumbala, which you can see only if you are willing to walk several miles across country. Quite a number of tribal people have become Christians.

Mary Esther has been active in the TB public health program of the hospital. When she completes the work of visiting in the homes, we will have some valuable medical and sociological information about the people among whom we live. Already one of the most appalling discoveries is the large number of Muslim women who have been divorced or abandoned by their husbands.

1968

Our children are growing up quickly. Miriam is being confirmed this year and will enter high school with the new school year. David will be starting his last year of high school in June and is already gathering information for college. Jimmy is active in sixth grade and has special interest in Boy Scouts. Joel is in third grade and sends letters that are getting more interesting all along. We are looking forward to seeing them during our vacation next month.

Hank is away from Wandoor several times a year on assignments from the IELC and the Henry Martyn Institute of Islamic Studies. We are also beginning an outreach in Perugamanna, a neglected area some 12 miles from Wandoor. During a recent festival there, we sold more than 900 pieces of Christian literature in one evening.

The Third Decade
1970

Another year has rolled around, and we are back in India after our furlough in 1969. After living in rural Wandoor since 1951, we have become city folks again and are back in Calicut. But there has been a greater change in our lives. Our family no longer includes six members but only five. Our third child, James Martyn, died at the boarding home in Kodaikanal on September 12th at fourteen years of age of a suspected cerebral hemorrhage connected with a kidney infection.

When Jimmy died Mary Esther was in Wandoor and I was in Malappuram, having just returned from a church meeting. We arrived at Kodaikanal early the next morning and joined Miriam and Joel, our other two children studying at Kodaikanal, in mourning and receiving comfort. Now Jim's body lies in the cemetery at Kodaikanal awaiting resurrection morning. Meanwhile we have been experiencing the comfort Christ has promised to those who mourn. We thank all of you who sent sympathy cards and condolence letters.

This summer we are looking forward to a visit from our oldest son David, now in his second year of college in America.

1972

India is moving into the industrial age very quickly. You may wonder how all this fits in with popular pictures of India that include holy cows, cobras, weird religious ceremonies, etc. Some of those things are still here, but they are by no means the main interest of the country. Rapid social change, restlessness, conflict between capital and labor, cross currents of various political philosophies and rising expectations all form the background for mission work in India today. The days when a missionary was often regarded as a dispenser of bounties from a more progressive part of the world are quickly disappearing. Why are we here? What can we do? The world may regard us as excess baggage, but we know the Gospel is the power of God unto salvation.

For a few months this year we had an entirely different type of work than we have had so far in India — houseparents at the boarding home for missionary children in Kodaikanal. The whole experience gave us a new appreciation for the service of the houseparents. We were intensely active from early morning to late at night. Leading the worship, teaching a Bible class for adults and helping prepare a group of children for confirmation gave Hank a taste of pastoral ministry once again.

Mary Esther is working on two literary projects aimed at presenting the Gospel to Muslims more effectively. One project is the translation of a book called *Face the Facts* into Malayalam. The book was written by a missionary in Singapore and is designed to help Muslim inquirers understand the Christian faith and overcome the most common objections. The second project involves revising a correspondence course on Luke. Translation is not easy because phrases that sound weighty and meaningful in English are often difficult to render into another language.

Miriam graduated from high school in May and spent the summer months with us in Calicut. On August 21 she and Alice Lutz started out for the United States, arriving in Boston four days later. Hank's folks took her to St. Olaf College, where she enrolled as a freshman nursing student. She likes the college and appreciates the many opportunities to hear good music there.

David is in his senior year at the Massachusetts Institute of Technology, busy working on his thesis project and helping support himself by managing one of the cafeterias. He is planning to take some post-graduate work next year. Joel, our youngest, is in eighth grade at the Kodaikanal boarding school.

1973

Along with encouraging individuals, the work of general outreach goes on. Just now several teams of Christian workers are conducting Bible correspondence course camps at high schools in this area. A few days ago a pastor in Calicut reported that more than 300 students had purchased a Gospel and received the first lesson. After only a few days 75 students had finished the course.

Last year we wrote about a Malayalam translation of a book called *Face the Facts.* It was finally printed under the Malayalam title *If This Is Your Question.* The first edition of 2,000 copies has been completely sold out.

1974

Early May marked one of the highlights of our year: a five-day retreat for Muslim inquirers in Calicut. It was a faith-strengthening experience not only for the inquirers but also for the staff.

Mary Esther's involvement in literature production continued in the early part of the year and also on our furlough. A second edition of *If This Is Your Question* in 2,000 copies has come off the press. In the past months she has arranged the reprinting of three booklets: *Heart of Tampi, Who is This Man?* and *Two Cities,* the first two in editions of 50,000 and the latter of 20,000. The *Heart of Tampi* describes how sin is driven out of the heart when Christ comes in. *Who is This Man?* is an attractive overview of the life of Christ, and *Two Cities* is a description of the way to eternal life.

Our furlough was busy. We saw David graduate from MIT with his master's degree in electrical engineering. We spent the early part of the summer with Hank's folks in Minneapolis. After an enjoyable reunion and vacation with Mary Esther's brothers and their families at an isolated lake in Ontario, we moved into a missionary home in St. Paul. Hank took some courses at nearby Luther Seminary for one quarter. He has been speaking at various church groups in Ohio, Maryland, Minnesota, Illinois, South Dakota, Iowa, New York, Wisconsin, Kansas and Oklahoma — 69 messages at 39 places.

1975

The highlight of the year was the baptism of Abdul Rahiman, his wife Aisha, their two children, and P. P. Alavi on June 15th in Malappuram. The period after baptism is often a traumatic one for converts from Islam. In addition to being ostracized from their own family and friends, they are often received with less than warmth by members of the church. That is one reason why it is good if the whole family can be baptized together; they can be of encouragement to each other. Happily, this group seems to be making a good adjustment.

Mary Esther is getting ready for printing a third edition of *If This is Your Question* and arranging for the distribution of three booklets printed previously. Now she is getting requests to put those works into the Karanese language. She is also checking manuscripts for the Scripture Gift Mission and preparing a Bible correspondence course on Luke's Gospel for more advanced students.

Hank is still connected with the Henry Martyn Institute of Islamic Studies and has helped give lectures and lead discussions on Islam and the Christian approach to Muslims for seminary students and Christian groups in Bombay, Sholapur, Hyderabad, Bangalore and Kottayam.

1976

This will probably be the last time we will be writing you from this address. Our landlord has given this house to his nephew as a wedding gift. Like most cities in India, Calicut is growing and has a housing shortage. We don't expect to find another place on the seashore like this one.

Our friends, Roland and Mary Helen Miller, left India in January. That not only brought pains of parting but affected our own work considerably. Mary Helen was active in a civic woman's organization in Malappuram. One of the projects of this group is the production and distribution of a special food supplement for children. Mary Esther has "inherited" Mary Helen's role as project advisor.

After numerous delays, the House of Hope for Muslim inquirers and converts in Meenangadi was finally completed and dedicated on June 17th. Two Muslim inquirers were the first guests and students. Although Hank had to discontinue

his formal relationship as Associate Director of the Henry
Martyn Institute because of increased work in the IELC, he
had the opportunity to help prepare several groups for witness
among the Muslims.

The outstanding event in our family during the past year
was the August marriage of our daughter Miriam to Vichian
Vilimpotchpornkul. Vichian is a young man from Thailand
Miriam knew in high school. After their graduation both of
them went to the United States, Miriam for studies in nursing
and Vichian in the field of economics. Miriam wrote the nursing state board exams in Minnesota in the middle of July and
then came out to India. Vichian came shortly before the wedding along with our oldest son David and two of his friends
from Boston. It was a happy time for all of us. Some of the missionaries joined the children in forming a choir and singing
"Jesu, Joy of Man's Desiring" for the wedding. After the wedding Miriam and Vichian spent some time in India and then
went to Thailand for about a month. Now they are back in the
States looking for some place to settle down.

1977

We finally moved at the end of June this year. It took
quite a while to find a suitable place, but in the end
the extra wait was worth it. We found a new house closer to
the center of Calicut, near one of the main roads but off a bit
on a quiet lane. The house is smaller than what we had
before, but we don't need so much space anymore.

We are actually writing from Minneapolis. We left India on
furlough at the beginning of September, arriving in Boston in
time for our son David's wedding. Afterward we drove to
Philadelphia and spent a week with Miriam and Vichian.
Several hundred miles and many visits later we stopped to see
Joel at Miami University in Oxford, Ohio, where he is starting
out as a student of architecture.

We are expecting to return to India at the end of the year
and again take up the work in the Malabar area.

1978

Several of you have written since you discovered that I was back in the States undergoing treatment for rheumatoid arthritis. After trying several oral medications, I am now receiving "gold therapy." I have three weekly shots of the gold salt — two at the hospital and one from the doctor's office. We are trying to find someone in India familiar with the treatment. I am eager to get back to India.

The Fourth Decade

1980

By the grace of God, Mary Esther was able to return to India, greatly improved, the first week of February. Her gold salt injections have been reduced to once every three weeks. She is able to do most of the things she did before the arthritis began.

We suffered two personal losses this year. Late in February Hank's brother Paul was killed when a semi-trailer truck struck his car from the rear when it was stopped at a railway crossing. Barely a month after Paul's accident Hank's dad died of heart failure. Hank made a quick trip to the States to spend a little time with his mother and help make plans for her future.

The House of Hope project for Muslim inquirers and converts is in a state of flux. The building is lying vacant, but we're sure the church here will find some other use for it. We're thinking of a girls' hostel and clinic. Mary Esther was invited to start a Bible study at the Malabar Christian College near our house. Hank is involved with various committees and activities of the IELC and the Henry Martyn Institute.

Hank woke up one morning with palpitation, but it subsided. Next morning we went to a retreat center. In the evening Hank took one of the lecturers to the bus station. Coming home he began to feel pain in his chest and left arm. The doctor advised Hank to stay in bed. The next day the doctor did an EKG, said it was a heart attack and sent Hank to the hospital, where he stayed for ten days. We were planning a short furlough at the end of May, but the doctor insisted we could not leave before the end of June. In the States Hank was examined by a cardiologist who thought Hank's condition was very favorable and encouraged him to get more exercise.

1981

Arabic is the religious language of Muslims everywhere. Even though their daily language may be Malayalam (as in our area), they learn Arabic from childhood. In religion classes they learn Arabic terms for Gospel and Jesus but do not find out about the salvation that comes through Jesus. For that we have been sent, and we know we are simply earthen vessels — Hank with heart limitations and Mary Esther with rheumatoid arthritis.

Here in Calicut we have had special joy working with individuals doing evangelism among college students. A home has been serving as the center for the work. Mary Esther supplies them with literature and encouragement; Hank sometimes helps out with a message and film presentation at their gatherings. The best hope for future evangelization of India may come from this work with students.

1982

We are writing from Minneapolis, where we have been staying with Miriam and her husband since July. We hope to return to India in mid-1983. The Lord has sustained Mary Esther through two operations. The first involved getting a new steel and plastic joint on her right knee, and the second involved work on her right wrist. We appreciate the support of our children and friends so much; there is much cause for joy and thanksgiving. Your prayers are being answered.

1983

Events of the past year ran the gamut of emotion — reunions with children, mother and friends; the death of

Hank's mother at 89; the birth of our first grandchild, Ahnate James Lim, to Miriam and Vichian; Mary Esther's two knee operations in April and her crushing fall in June that resulted in a broken hip and our delayed return to India; some 90 presentations on the work among the Muslims in India by Hank; and finally reunion with friends and fellow missionaries in India. We are awaiting word of the birth of our second grandchild to David and Laurie.

The new Friendship Centre building in Calicut financed by the LCMS Manitoba-Saskatchewan District is nearing completion. The mission had been using a rented building for worship, parsonage, Bible correspondence course centre and nursery school since 1964. The new three-story building has sufficient space for all of our present activities; it has a good location with several large educational institutions nearby and is in a part of town where there are no other Christian churches.

Hank's book on the Ahmadiyya doctrine of God was published by the Henry Martyn Institute. The Ahmadiyyas are a sect of Islam that started about the turn of the century. One of their distinctive teachings is that Jesus did not die at the time of the crucifixion but merely fainted and later revived to travel to Kashmir, where he lived to a ripe age and died a natural death. The Ahmadiyyas have a group here in Calicut; they have been buying a number of copies of the book, but we have not been able to ascertain their reaction.

We ask your prayers for our own health. Mary Esther is much improved in her knees but still has arthritis in her hands, ankles and other joints. She walks without help on the level but uses crutches for going up and down stairs. Hank has to guard against overexertion. We are thankful that we were able to return to India, and pray God's grace in Christ may still reach others through our being here.

P.S. James Stewart Otten was born to David and Laurie in November.

1984

We visited the nursery school yesterday. There are two teachers and 65 pupils, the majority of whom are from Muslim homes. The enthusiastic greetings and smiling faces of the children were in sharp contrast to the weeping and wailing of opening day when many of the children left home for the first time.

Mary Esther has been continuing work on the project of supplying high-protein food for children. The women in charge have been concentrating on marketing the food on a retail basis under the name *Bala Poshini* (Nourishment for Children). After a lot of frustration and delays, the first packages are now on the shelves of several shops.

Recently Mary Esther received a list of more than 200 names and addresses of Muslims who have responded to a new Christian broadcast in the Malayalam language called "Heavenly Voice." We want to send them the correspondence course, "God's Good News for You."

There has been a lot of violence in India this year, culminating in the tragic assassination of Indira Gandhi in October and the subsequent communal outbreaks that followed. The new leader of India, Rajiv Gandhi, certainly needs our prayers.

1985

By now many of you may have heard that Hank suffered a fatal heart attack on February 22 while at a meeting in Madras. Hank had left for Madras on the train with nurse Betty Mayer the previous afternoon. They stayed overnight at the home of Arnold and Juanita Lutz. After breakfast the next morning, Hank felt uncomfortable and said he wished to lie down. When he went to get up, he collapsed on the floor. Betty tried to resuscitate him but to no avail.

Dr. Victoria Matthews brought the news to me. Just a short time before that, the postman had brought the mail. In it was an Easter card from a family in St. Louis. I thought that odd since it is still a month until Easter. After I received the news from Dr. Victoria, it flashed through my mind that the Lord was already confirming to me the message of the resurrection. Some friends here thought Hank might have wanted to be buried at Kodaikanal since Jimmy is buried there. But I knew it was Hank's wish to be buried in Wandoor. We choose a spot beside the church.

Dr. Victoria stayed with me through the night. People from many places started for Wandoor as soon as they heard the news. It was broadcast over All-India radio here in Kerala and also was in the two Malayalam papers early Saturday morning. Most of the missionary families were able to come. A short service was held at the small bungalow where I was staying. After that the pall bearers carried the casket in procession over to the hospital compound. Thousands of people were waiting there, local people as well as IELC pastors and others from all over. At the service Rev. K. M. Victor beautifully preached the Gospel. Singing of hymns and lyrics went on throughout. The committal was read by Rev. John Huss, IELC president.

Many people had been blessed by Hank's simple but profound witness, both in word and in deed. All were bearing witness to his gentle ways and his love in action for all he met. Most of the shops in town were closed for the day out of respect. Schools were closed in the afternoon. Someone said he had never seen such a vast crowd of people assembled for any meeting in Wandoor.

David came to India to be with me. Daily people come to offer their sympathy. May the resurrection victory of our Lord Jesus Christ confirm to you the promise that all those in Christ will experience the same victory! Hank is just one step ahead of us.

Even though I longed to rush home to my family after Hank's death, there were many things to be done. Our rented house needed to be vacated. Books and files from the beginning of our work till the present had to be dealt with. Betty Mayer spent several days and nights each week helping me.

Joel made plans to be with me during the last month in India, and he pitched right in and worked very hard. Joel and I left Calicut on May 26. We went to Minneapolis, where I stayed with Miriam and her family. On June 22 a memorial service was held at Mt. Calvary Lutheran Church.

Mary Esther recovering from hand and foot surgery

In July we made a trip to Grand Rapids, Michigan, to consult a hand surgeon, Dr. Swanson, about surgery to help my rheumatoid arthritis deformities. We settled on surgery for the right hand and the left foot on August 26. Rev. Rodney Otto, pastor of St. Mark Lutheran Church in Grand Rapids, shared my need with his congregation. One family became "my family," and I stayed in their home. I had hoped to return to India in late October but knew I wasn't ready to go, so I delayed the trip.

Some of you will wonder at my plan to return to India. But I think those who have known me best are not surprised. It is only natural since for the last 35 years India has been our home. I am not able to cope with the fast pace of American life because of my handicaps. I think I have more things I can do in India than here. I can get help for the physical support needed and have time for literature work and Gospel ministry. I may not know what the future holds, but I know Who holds my future. Please continue to pray for the work among the Muslims in India. There is much to be done and the laborers are few.

1986

I am back in India. Nurse Betty Mayer is getting ready to leave for her retirement and it seemed suitable for me to employ Maggie, Betty's helper, as my helper. My first purpose in coming back to India was to organize the historical material that had been in our files all these years. Secondly, I wanted to continue to use the gifts many of you had sent for our work here. Thirdly, I just want to live here and interact with local people, our pastors and evangelists, and whoever the Lord sends my way.

A number of projects are in varying stages of completion. Let me list them for you: a much needed three-day retreat for our pastors in the Malabar mission circle; vacation Bible schools in 21 places involving some 839 children, of whom more than 500 were non-Christians; and repair of the chapel roof in one place where termites were destroying all the roof beams. The hospital, too, is in desperate need of repairs, and we are trying to tackle them as funds become available.

We printed 150,000 booklets for evangelism last year and have a similar amount at press now. Ten thousand more copies of our Bible correspondence course Book I, "God's Good News for You," recently came off the press; 5,000 copies of a second course called "Promises of God" are now ready. We are interested in conducting camps near high schools, where students can enroll in the course and complete it in five or six days.

Many local people come and wonder if I have time to spend with them. How nice to be able to say, "I have no agenda; if God sent you here, then my time today is for you!" Wandoor

Mary Esther with friends in Wandoor

is a small town off the beaten path, but I am amazed how many of my Christian friends turn up here. Muslim friends we knew many years ago come too.

Miriam gave birth to a healthy baby girl on March 4th. They named her Pareena, a Thai name. Her nickname is Champoo, which means "pink." Miriam and Vichian and the children moved to Bangkok in August. Vichian is helping his mother and two brothers in the family business.

I must tell you about Christmas in Wandoor, this time with no family members around. First the question was asked; "Will we have a carol group?" Many were ready to answer "yes," but who would lead it? Finally a young man was willing to take charge. A group of 12 to 20 young men went each night to a different area around Wandoor, singing the good news of Jesus' birth. On December 21 a special Christmas program was planned at Tiruvally. The carol group provided special songs. The program went until 3:00 a.m. the next day! On December 22 a special Christmas program was held at Pergamanna, but I did not go because the chapel there is not accessible by car. December 23 was set for our hospital staff Christmas dinner. Some 65 people, including staff and children, were present. Huge cooking pots were set on three piles of brick in the backyard and firewood put underneath. The traditional festival food called *biriyani* was good! Christmas Eve, as in many parts of the world, is the children's Christmas program. Here it is the highlight of our celebration. Following our Christmas Day worship, we ate dinner to the accompaniment of Bach's Christmas Oratorio and a wealth of other traditional Christmas music.

1987

Greetings once again from South India. I am thankful that the Lord has permitted me to write to you from this place once again. By March of this year, walking had become increasingly difficult with my new left prosthesis. So I sent an S.O.S. to Joel, and he arrived here on May 5. We returned together to the States, where I had surgery. All went well. During physical therapy I noticed my walking was rather like limping. An x-ray showed much arthritis in both hips. The doctor advised I spend a month recuperating and then return for a total hip replacement. The second operation was performed on August 5.

Mary Esther and daughter Miriam in India

Miriam arrived from Thailand on October 16 and things swung into high gear. We left for Thailand on November 7. What a joy to visit with her husband Vichian and the children, Ahnate and Champoo. Champoo is one-and-a-half and this was the first time I had seen her. It was so nice to hear her say "Grandma." Miriam flew to India with me and spent three weeks before returning to Thailand.

Two matters are a cause of joy here in India: the arrival of Mr. D. Appukuttan and family to work with us in Muslim evangelism in Wandoor and the way in which the hospital has developed over these past months. There is a new atmosphere of cooperation and unity that pervades the place.

1988

When I had my left hip replacement in August 1987, the doctor had seen the deterioration of both hips but expressed the hope that by doing one the other might slow down and not need to be replaced for a while. But already in March I began having trouble. Gradually some pain was developing in my knee. My friends, Roland and Mary Helen Miller, were in India at that time and offered to arrange a ticket for me on their flight. So I returned to the States and

Mary Esther visits with Roland Miller

had the hip surgery. Then on October 15 Joel and I left for Bangkok. We spent a week with Miriam and family. Joel returned to the States, and Miriam's husband went on to India with me.

Vacation Bible school was conducted in five sites around Wandoor, with some 200 children attending, including 35 Muslim children and 134 Hindu children. My literature ministry has continued. This has included 50,000 copies of a leaflet called "Have You Met ...?" and 10,000 copies of the booklet, *Who Is This Man?* This was possible through several gifts, including one large gift from the Lutheran Women of Great Britain.

This letter does not really deal with the heart of our work — the daily contact with individuals who will judge the reliability of the Gospel and be drawn to the Savior by what they see and hear from us.

1989

You are correct to deduce that Mrs. Otten is not moving as rapidly as she would like. Hips and knees have been made "new," but ankles are now the latest to feel the effect of rheumatoid arthritis. There doesn't seem to be a good surgery for ankles.

David, Laurie and their son Jimmy and Laurie's parents, Dr. and Mrs. G. Stewart, visited in October. We all went up to

Kodaikanal to visit the school and surroundings where our children spent so much of their "India lives." And now, to put the icing on the cake, I have Miriam and Champoo here with me for three weeks over Christmas. Vichian, who teaches college, and first-grader Ahnate don't have vacation now, so they had to stay in Bangkok.

There is an upsurge of concern on the part of many Christians to reach out to the world's vast Muslim population. We are praising God for this. Even in the United States and Canada there are many opportunities. I would like to encourage you to check out your own neighborhood; find out what Muslims believe and learn how to befriend them. Join hands with us.

Mary Esther at work at her desk

The Fifth Decade

1991

I am writing from Minneapolis. I had an appointment with my orthopedic surgeon on December 10, and he concluded I was a suitable candidate for an ankle implant. The operation went well, and I was ready to leave the hospital on Christmas Eve and enter rehab for 17 days. Now the cast has been removed. The doctor is pleased with the results.

For a long time I have wanted to revise a Malayalam translation of the life story of Dr. Sa'eed of Iran. We finally were able to complete that and the manuscript is at press. Christian literature continues to be one of our best ways to communicate the Gospel in our part of India.

1992

I am back in Minneapolis again. I had a broken tooth in India so I visited a dentist. He noticed an ulcer on my tongue. He pulled the broken tooth but said if the ulcer did not heal within a month other investigations would be necessary. I went back five weeks later. The ulcer was 50 percent better, but the dentist wasn't satisfied. He called in a friend, a maxillo-facial surgeon, who recommended a biopsy. The pathology report: "Squamous cell carcinoma." He assured me it is a slow-growing type of cancer and we were getting it early. He thought I should go to the States as soon as possible. Maggie went with me on the train to Madras, where Miriam arrived about midnight by plane. We flew to Bangkok, and Joel was waiting there.

In the States I was examined by several doctors and, after hearing the "pitch" from both sides (radiation and surgery), I felt the best way for me would be with surgery. By doing surgery the nodes can be dissected at the same time and biopsied. If any cancer cells are found, radiation might also be necessary.

Only a few people in India know the reason for my sudden trip home. God willing, I hope to return to India once more. How true it is that we never know what tomorrow will bring, but how wonderful to have the assurance that we are in the safe and loving hands of our Heavenly Father.

Endings

Mary Esther's last days in retrospect as written by her son David:

December 4, 1993

Dear Friends,

For those of you who have not heard, I have the sad task of informing you of the death of my mother, Mary Esther

Otten, on October 9, 1993, from cancer and complications of her arthritis. She was staying with my family and me at our home. Both Miriam and Joel were here when she died. Her memorial service was held at our church. Long-time friends and coworkers of my parents, Rev. Roland Miller and his wife Mary Helen, came from Minneapolis for the service and Rev. Miller gave the address. My mother is buried in a cemetery near our house, which is the resting place of a number of missionaries to India.

My mother's last form letter was dated January 6, 1993. At that time she was in the States after an operation on her tongue. On January 23 she headed back to India with Joel via Thailand. Soon after reaching India, Mother started to complain about numbness in her left hand and arm. Writing by hand was difficult, but she was able to type. By the end of March, her left hand and arm were so weak she could only type with her right hand. By the beginning of May, she could not walk or stand. She went to Calicut to her orthopedic surgeon. Since the prognosis was poor, Mother wanted to stay on in India for three or four months to wind up some of her projects.

During this time Rev. Miller came to India on other business and visited my mother. Shortly before he arrived she came down with a cold, which turned into a lung infection, which turned into a breathing arrest. Maggie, Mom's servant, immediately went to the hospital for help. Emergency treatment was successful and Mom revived. Everyone was very shook up by the incident, but Mother still wanted to stay in India until she could terminate her affairs in a more satisfactory way. Rev. Miller flew back via Thailand, where he talked with Miriam, and Minneapolis, where he talked with Joel. This was the first time anyone outside India realized my mother's health had deteriorated so much. We decided Miriam should visit Mom in India on her way to a course she was taking in Vermont over the summer.

On June 30 Mom had a CT scan of her neck. The results showed that in addition to the original problem there was a malignant tumor on the side of Mom's neck. It was untreatable. Knowing her condition was terminal, Mom was more determined to stay in India as long as she was able to contribute there. Joel stayed until the middle of August. I came several days before Joel left and stayed until the end of August. Several days before I left Miriam arrived and stayed for almost two more weeks.

Mother spent most of her waking hours in her wheelchair. She could read if someone turned the pages for her, but talking with people was what she did most. Many people came to see her, some just to visit, some for advice, some for financial help and some to report on what they were doing. Although she was paralyzed from the neck down, she was still able to be a source of strength and fellowship to many people.

During this time there were three main projects Mother was interested in finishing. The Luke Bible correspondence course was the first. A week before she left India the press delivered 5,000 copies of the course to her living room. One of the last things we did was to organize the distribution of this literature. A second project was the Henry Otten English Medium School located on the hospital compound. The school needs government recognition so more grades can be added. Mother was instrumental in expanding the board of directors to provide more energy and resources for this endeavor. The third project was the compound in Wynad. This valuable property has been managed for many years by Mr. P. K. George and his family. The conversion of this property into a possible school for inquirers is a task that was turned over to Alice Brauer. Fortunately the hospital has a very capable and hard-working medical superintendent in Dr. Rao and an excellent OB-GYN in Dr. Leelavathi. Mother often said that though these two were Hindus, the care and compassion they showed for the patients was often greater than that of the Christian staff.

Throughout the summer all of us children had been pleading with Mother to set a date for coming to the States or going to Thailand. It was increasingly difficult to take care of her, and we worried about what would happen if she were very sick for a long time. Moving her took two people and was required many times during the day and night. Mother finally agreed that Miriam and I should bring her to my home at the beginning of October. We sold all of Mother's furniture, gave away most of her books and went through every barrel, trunk, closet and cabinet making sure everything was given or sold to the person who could use it best or appreciate it most. When we left, the house looked quite bare with only the mission furniture left.

The trip to the States was quite difficult. Everyone was glad when we finally got to Boston. My wife Laurie had turned our dining room into a cozy little bedroom complete with a hospital bed. She had also arranged to have a hospice nurse and member of our church, Marilyn Harder, at the house when Mom arrived. Marilyn was invaluable during the next few days, helping to make Mom comfortable and giving us a chance to catch our breath. Having accomplished what she wanted to in India, Mom faded fast once she reached the States. We arrived Tuesday, October 5, and by Wednesday evening she was in serious pain. Thursday we hooked up with a doctor who was able to prescribe some pain medication that made her more comfortable. Joel arrived Friday from Minneapolis and Mom was able to see him. When he left India earlier in the summer, neither he nor Mom thought they would see each other again on this earth. Saturday night Mother passed away.

In closing I would like to say how proud I am of my mother, her lifetime of commitment to her work on the mission field and her complete disregard for personal comfort and convenience. I feel truly privileged to have had the opportunity to serve her this past summer and to help make her last days in India as useful and productive as possible. While Miriam, Joel and I do not live close together, it was great to work and laugh together one more time as a family.

An era may have ended when my mother left India, but the work begun through her continues on. Many others are still spreading the Good News. Please remember the hospital and its staff, the school and its teachers, and all the evangelists in your prayers.

Sincerely,
David Otten

Ruby Young, a former public school teacher, has contributed articles to the Lutheran Woman's Quarterly. *She lives in Tulsa, Oklahoma, with her husband Rufus. They have four grown children.*